Crooked Brooklyn

Also by Michael Vecchione

Friends of the Family

Also by Jerry Schmetterer

The Godplayer

The Coffey Files: One Cop's War Against the Mob

The King of Clubs: The Story of Scores

E-Man: Life in the NYPD Emergency Service Unit

Crooked Brooklyn

Taking Down Corrupt Judges, Dirty Politicians, Killers, and Body Snatchers

MICHAEL VECCHIONE
and JERRY SCHMETTERER

THOMAS DUNNE BOOKS ST. MARTIN'S PRESS NEW YORK

THOMAS DUNNE BOOKS.
An imprint of St. Martin's Press.

www.thomasdunnebooks.com
www.stmartins.com

Designed by Steven Seighman

Library of Congress Cataloging-in-Publication Data

ISBN 978-1-250-06518-6 (hardcover)
ISBN 978-1-4668-7174-8 (e-book)

First Edition: November 2015

10 9 8 7 6 5 4 3 2 1

To Mom and Dad, everything I am I owe to you. Dad, you lived a long and wonderful life, and to this day I can hear your words "always do the right thing."

To Pam, my wonderful sister, I know you are always with me. I miss you and will always love you.

To Brian and Andrew, you make me proud to be your dad. I love you both.

To Lenor, thank you for your trust, your support, your loyalty, and your love. God was smiling down on me the day I met you. Ti amo!

—MV

To the grandboys, Isaac Malcolm Schmetterer, Carston Joris Alaimo, and Austen Elijah Schmetterer

—JS

Contents

Crooked Brooklyn

Prologue

I KNEW IT AS SOON as we got in the elevator. This was what I wanted. I was on the way to a real live crime scene. A man jumped or got pushed out of the fifth-floor window of a luxury apartment building not far from the offices of the Brooklyn district attorney.

I was a first-year assistant in the Investigations Bureau. My briefcase hardly had a wrinkle in it, about one week since I'd passed the bar exam. Now, I had been summoned by a veteran, topflight assistant district attorney, Joe Lauria, a homicide prosecutor, to join him on a "ride." He was responding to a call from the police that the DA was needed at the scene.

"The vic is a guy named Robert Morse. He is the US Attorney for the Eastern District of New York. Cops tell me he has something to do with the Watergate investigation," Lauria had said matter-of-factly as we headed to the elevator.

Watergate, I thought. *It's the biggest story in the country right now. Am I going to be involved in it?*

I urged the elevator to go faster. When we finally hit the street, I almost started to run. I knew where the scene was, just a few blocks west in one of the finest neighborhoods in the city.

Lauria practically grabbed me to slow me down. He was totally cool, walking to see a body as if it were another stroll along the nearby Brooklyn Heights promenade. I wondered why he even wanted me along. But I didn't care. It was a bright sunny day, warm for December. The streets were packed with shoppers, and the trendy restaurants filled with diners. I had no idea that at the end of the street a body was waiting for Michael F. Vecchione, wet-behind-the-ears assistant from the Brooklyn District Attorney's Office.

From a block away we could see the flashing lights of the police who had blocked off the street with yellow tape. We saw a long line of unmarked police cars, those with the red-cherry lights on the roof.

"A lot of brass here, Feds too," Lauria mentioned.

I had no idea who the Feds were.

As we got closer, I felt like I was walking onto a movie set and I was the star. I fell in behind my mentor as he approached a sergeant keeping the sidewalk clear. I fumbled to clip my ID card on my jacket pocket.

Lauria, who had an actual gold shield, did not bother to display it. The cops seemed to recognize him and waved us both through. I couldn't be happier. This is what Detective First Grade Jimmy Murphy, my then-wife's uncle, used to tell me about. It was the major leagues: crime, New York, Brooklyn, being in a position where people looked to you to do something about it.

Inside the police line was the body, covered with a sheet. It stopped me in my tracks. It looked like you see in movies. A body covered by a sheet, people wearing badges and Windbreakers taking pictures, standing around writing in small notebooks, whispering to each other. On one of the jackets it said FBI CRIME SCENE *Oh, the Feds,* I realized.

The dead man, the US Attorney for the Eastern District of New York, had been appointed by President Nixon. Lauria was an assistant Kings County district attorney. He worked for the county. His boss was the Brooklyn district attorney, local. I was a member of the bar for one week—a nobody. But here I was, assisting in the investigation of a man who was connected to the Watergate conspiracy.

Lauria took me by the elbow and led me closer to the body. Outside of a funeral home, I had never before been so close to a dead man. Lauria knelt down close to the head and lifted the sheet. I looked over his shoulder. It struck me like a sleeping man who had lain down in a pool of blood. I was frozen, afraid to get closer. Over the years I would become accustomed to being near, even examining, dead bodies. That moment I was frozen in time, not knowing what to do or what to say. Lauria dropped the sheet back in place.

We went into the building, the nicest lobby I had ever seen. It was packed with people, I assumed building residents, and some wearing badge-shaped cards around their necks reading WORKING PRESS.

They seemed to know Lauria and called out for him to stop for a second. "Lauria, what's this about? Was he pushed? Give us a second!" they shouted. He tried not to look at them as he muttered under his breath, "Fucking vultures. Michael, stay away from them. They will do you no good."

At the fifth floor the hallway was packed to saturation with men in dark suits, white shirts, and striped ties. We had to push our way through into the apartment, which was almost as packed. I struggled to appear cool, calm, and collected, but under my cheap suit I was sweating profusely.

An older man, someone I recognized from the newspapers, approached us. He leaned close to Lauria's ear and half whispered something about finding a note and a woman's being involved. Lauria shook his hand and muttered, "Thanks, Chief." It struck me that this was the chief of detectives of the NYPD.

The crowd parted a little and let Lauria and me approach the open window. They parted for us. I was relaxing a little, enjoying the feeling of importance. Truthfully, I was loving every minute of it.

Lauria stood at the window, looked out, then looked back into the room. Next he leaned out, checking the sill, careful not to touch the fingerprint powder that seemed to be all around the frame. When he leaned out again, a flash went off from a camera across the street. This was big-time stuff; press photographers were on the roof across the street, and television live trucks were beginning to arrive.

Lauria stepped back into the center of the room. "I'll need a copy of that note as soon as possible," he told a detective. We, Lauria and I, gave an order to a cop. All the eyes in the room were on us. And they were respectful. They saw us as professionals, just as my uncle Louie Longobardi used to tell me: "A lawyer is a respected man. It's honorable and can be very exciting."

Uncle Louie and Jimmy Murphy had convinced me to go to law school. They didn't talk about the money you could make or the security of a government job. They told me about the stature, the importance, the satisfaction of putting bad guys away. Here on my most exciting day yet on the job, I found out they were right.

By the time Lauria and I headed back to the office, I knew I'd made the right decision. Walking back through that crowd in the street, I was a foot taller than when I'd walked in.

About an hour after we got back to the office, a cop arrived with a copy of the suicide note. Lauria called me into his small office and let me see it. The dead man had written that he'd contemplated suicide in the past. He'd seen a psychiatrist about it. He said he was involved in a difficult love affair. The note was rambling and incoherent. Nothing indicated that his death was prompted by anything other than personal problems.

Lauria called the chief of detectives. The police shared his analysis. He then called District Attorney Eugene Gold and told him his findings. That was it. No murder, nothing more for us to do but fill out a report for the DA.

"Thanks for your help, kid," Lauria said as he buried his face in his typewriter to do the report.

I went back home from there. I could not wait to tell my wife about the special day I'd just completed. I talked her ears off. I was too pumped up, too excited, to even think about going to bed. I called my dad, my uncles, my best friends, everyone else

I could reach, and repeated the events of the day. They all did not get what I was so over-the-top about, but I explained, "This is great, I am in."

The next day the suicide was the lead story in all the newspapers and television news shows. When I got to work, I continued to bore anyone who would listen with the events of the previous night.

Then Lauria came to get me again: "Hey, Mike, wanna go to a mob rubout?"

A few minutes later we were on our way to a social club alongside the Gowanus Canal where a notorious mobster had just been blown away.

I was hooked. This was the life for me.

Chapter 1

Someone Wants Me Dead

You really need to work on your threats. I can't tell if you are threatening me or inviting me for tea.

—Ilona Andrews

"Someone wants you dead," George barked into the phone. "Get up here right away."

I laughed into the phone. "You're full of it!"

I was sitting comfortably at my desk about halfway through a trial transcript, reluctant to put it down, but when George called, people listened.

"No, it's no joke, it can't wait! Someone wants to kill you! Get up here," George insisted.

Supervising Detective Investigator George Terra was a serious guy, and by *up here* I understood he wanted me to come to his conference room on the eighteenth floor, one above me, in a well-secured part of the building. Many of the biggest cases in the office of the Kings County district attorney had their roots in that small conference room.

It's not every day that you hear that someone wants to kill you, even for a homicide prosecutor who sometimes sends killers to the chair. On the way to the elevator I ran over some of the possible suspects. I thought of Benny Geritano's mother. I sent him away for ten years. Previously, I had convicted his brother, her younger son. She had the right to hate me. She had stood in the courtroom and cursed me out. I never took it seriously. DAs hear that all time. But her family had the connections to make it happen. Her late husband was a Mafia enforcer who was killed when he went to collect money owed to mob kingpin John Gotti and the mark got the jump on him.

I walked into George's conference room, and sitting in a chair against the wall was an inmate. He was desperate looking and shifty with a pale complexion like he never spent a minute in the sun. The guy had *put me in jail* written all over him.

George started things off: "Mike, this guy asked to come here from Rikers to talk about a different case. Now he says he knows someone who wants you dead . . . putting out a contract. He wants to inform in exchange for a get-out-of-jail-free card." George, his ever-present toothpick swirling around his lips, never minced words.

George had seen it all. He was an accomplished undercover operative specializing in posing as a hit man. He looked Brooklyn, spoke Brooklyn, and dressed Brooklyn. His signature look was an untied tie around his neck knotted only when he appeared in court. If he was taking this guy seriously, then I needed to concentrate. A stranger was about to tell me who was willing to pay to see me dead.

"Tell him what you know," George said to the man, whose identity he had promised to protect. He would forever be known, in all paperwork pertaining to this case, as C.I., "confidential informant."

"Listen, I'm not bullshitting. I wouldn't fuck with you guys," C.I. began. "It's a guy named Demicco, he's a wiseguy, he's sitting in Rikers waiting for his ride upstate to do a stretch for manslaughter. Killed his sister's scumbag boyfriend seven years ago. He wants Vecchione hit. He thinks I'm getting out soon, offered me the contract, ten large. I told him I would think about it."

So I had my answer. Mike Demicco. A wiseguy, not someone I would have guessed would pay to have me killed. Wiseguys know how the game is played. They do their thing, we do our thing. They have their rules and we have ours. I was not sure exactly how to deal with this, but George was.

George already had a plan. First of all, he would assign detectives to guard me twenty-four hours a day. Then he would wire up C.I. and send him back to Rikers with the intention of getting Demicco to incriminate himself.

I heard George out but I was in kind of a fog. I was stunned. I certainly knew Demicco. He was a Colombo family associate, a tough character who knew the ropes. We gave him a pretty good plea, six to eighteen years. After a trial, he would have gotten twenty-five to life if convicted.

Karen Turner, a rookie assistant DA, and I had a good case against him for killing his sister's boyfriend, whose name was Carlos Beltram. We had strong forensic evidence and a codefendant who was eager to testify against Demicco. His story was fitting for an episode of *The Sopranos.* It began in 1995, about seven years prior to this meeting with C.I.

"Angelo," a Demicco henchman, had told us what had happened.

Demicco did not like the boyfriend. The kid was Puerto Rican, which right away was a strike against him with a connected family, and he was rough with the sister. And he was on parole following a drug bust. But, as these things go, she would not break up with him. True love, I guess.

Demicco took matters into his own hands. He told Beltram that he could get him a job with a company out in Sheepshead Bay. He offered to pick him up and drive him to the interview. Beltram agreed. Angelo stole a Cadillac limo and they picked up Beltram in Bushwick. Then they drove out along the Belt Parkway toward the supposed interview site.

Of course, along the way Angelo noticed something wrong with the car and pulled off the road and into a wooded area that is now Erskine Street, but back then was a few acres of scraggly woods and empty lots strewn with abandoned cars. Angelo popped the hood and asked Beltram to take a look with him to see what might be the trouble.

Beltram said, "Thank God. I thought this might be a hit," and that's when Demicco pulled a gun and ordered the boyfriend to walk into the woods. Angelo said he kept his head under the hood and pretended to be repairing something in case a Highway Patrol cop decided to check them out.

As Angelo told the story, after about two minutes of looking under the hood, he heard two shots. He figured the deed was done so he put the hood back in place and got behind the wheel. But five, then ten minutes, passed and Demicco did not return. Angelo decided to go looking for him.

As he got a few feet into the dense woods, Angelo was suddenly attacked by Beltram, who began to wrestle with him and beg for help. He promised he wouldn't go to the cops. While he struggled to get Beltram off him, Angelo noticed two bleeding holes in Beltram's chest. He had obviously been shot and was out of his mind with fear and rage. Just then Demicco appeared, carrying a small piece of lumber, which he quickly brought into contact with Beltram's skull.

It was a vicious beating. The younger man's fingers were torn off his hands in a vain effort to protect himself, and down he went. A few more smacks in the head from Demicco and the hapless Beltram was dead.

Next the two hoods had to bury the body. They had neglected to bring a shovel. Looking around for an alternative to a shallow grave, they spotted a sort of burial ground for discarded car tires. They dragged the boyfriend's body to the pile, and then, too exhausted to do much more, they merely covered it up with a few tires near the bottom of the stack.

About one week later, they returned to the scene of the crime with shovels, determined to give the boyfriend a proper burial. But what they found disgusted them so much they were paralyzed with fear and panic. Even seven years later when Angelo told the story, he broke into a sweat. He said when they removed the tires, all they found was rotting flesh and maggots crawling all over him, in his eyes, his mouth. "We almost puked," Angelo recounted, "so Mike said, 'Fuck this,' and threw the tires back on him and we split."

Then they learned that the tire burial ground was to be excavated to make way for a shopping-center complex. Demicco got Angelo, and once again with shovels they made their third visit to the fateful site.

This time all they found was a skeleton that had been picked clean by the maggots and other slimy things that live off dead bodies. So Demicco figured they could avoid the work of digging a grave. He shocked Angelo by grabbing the skeleton's head and snapping it off at the neck. Holding the skull in one hand, he punched out the front and most of the other teeth with his other fist. Only a few teeth in the rear of the skull remained. Then he took the skull and put it in a plastic bag he'd brought with him. He tied the bag and heaved it into the woods. Eventually it landed in a nearby creek. Then he and Angelo packed the remaining bones into five plastic bags, put them in the trunk, and took them to Bensonhurst, where they distributed the bags into Dumpsters throughout their neighborhood.

Four years later in 1999, the shopping center was built and the boyfriend's disappearance was an unsolved case that no one was trying too hard to crack, when an innocent fisherman working the stream across from Erskine Street hooked a plastic bag. When he opened, it he found a skull. He examined the find, then threw it away into the sickly stand of woods. Another fisherman saw this and called the police.

The medical examiner's office took possession of the skull and called in a forensic dentist and a forensic anthropologist.

They made some notes, noticing that the skull had been hit with a large object. With no one to connect the skull to, the report got filed away and the skull was buried in potter's field. No body, just the battered skull.

About two years after that I got a call from a friend in the NYPD Intelligence Unit. Angelo, now working off a federal gun-running charge, told him a story about his friend Mike Demicco, who had killed his sister's boyfriend. He said he knew this because he drove him to the crime scene. The detective learned that the case might involve a skull known to the medical examiner's office.

My friend asked if I wanted to pursue the case against Demicco. The old case had never been reported as a homicide, but if we could prove the skull belonged to the boyfriend, I thought we would have something to bring to a jury.

So, we retrieved the medical examiner's report, which mentioned the bashed-in skull—a testament to the great work those guys do—which matched Angelo's story of Demicco's beating the boyfriend to death with a piece of wood after his bullets failed to do the trick. But that would not be enough to convince anyone that it belonged to the boyfriend. We needed to match those remaining teeth. On a hunch I suggested we find out if the boyfriend ever did any time. Maybe he had dental work done in prison.

Sure enough, he did do time in state prison and visited the dentist while he was there. We found his prison dental records, and a forensic dentist—these guys are geniuses—using X-rays the medical examiner had on file, matched the boyfriend's teeth to those remaining in the skull.

In addition, we had the victim's brother testifying that Beltram was meeting Demicco to go on a job interview that day and was never seen again. Also, significantly, we had a tape of a telephone call Beltram's brother had the foresight to record when he first became concerned about his brother. On the tape, Demicco admitted he took Beltram to the job interview, then back to Bushwick, but didn't know what happened to him after that.

Demicco's defense was just that. In the face of the evidence we had, it was not an explanation any lawyer would want to take into court.

The grand jury bought the evidence and Angelo's story and returned an indictment for murder against Demicco.

Several months later, Demicco pled guilty to manslaughter with the promise of a six-to-eighteen-year sentence. If he was found guilty at trial, he might have faced twenty-five years to life. I let the rookie Karen Turner handle the sentencing. She stood at the prosecution table and gave the judge a rundown of the case and the evidence against Demicco, who sat sulking in his chair.

She reported for the record the deal we had struck. The defendant was sentenced by the judge. That was that.

I had an interesting case under my belt, and young Turner, who went on to become a stalwart of the Rackets Division, got some valuable face time with a supreme court judge, a real mobster, and his defense attorney.

Now I was hearing Demicco wanted to pay to have me killed. I didn't get it. He got caught fair and square. He was a mob associate, he lived by a certain code, and this did not fit in. I could understand if he wanted to kill Angelo for snitching on him, but I was doing my job.

Well, we had our C.I. to help us figure it out and perhaps trap Demicco into some new charges against him, such as conspiracy to murder a prosecutor. So George, working with the Department of Correction, the people who run the New York City jails, arranged for C.I. to go back to Rikers, where he would wear a wire when he met with Demicco and agree to take the contract for the hit.

Meanwhile I was living with the permanent shadows. District Attorney Charles J. Hynes assigned two female detectives as my primary bodyguards, and I would have protection twenty-four hours a day. I hated it. It drew attention to me everywhere I went. Not that I mind being in the spotlight, but not for those reasons.

One night after work, alone except for the two bodyguards, I headed to my favorite restaurant at the time, an Italian place on First Avenue in Manhattan. It is a famous hangout for law enforcement and media types. The rumor is that it was "silently" owned by Vincent "Chin" Gigante, the head of the Genovese crime family and the real "godfather" of New York crime.

I was at the bar nursing a scotch when the "owner" came over. He knew me as a regular and asked about the two women sitting on the bench in front of the restaurant.

He generously offered to bring them in. "On me, I'll treat them right," he said.

I filled him in on the situation, explaining they were doing their jobs by sitting out in front. He offered to help. "You know,

Mike, I can take care of this. I know some people who can make that contract go away."

I thanked him but told him it was all under control.

In the evenings two detectives were stationed in a car outside my father's home in Queens where I was living while he recovered from a stroke. The office security people were taking the threat seriously.

They even flagged the license plates of the cars of my two sons, Brian and Andrew, so they would be alerted if anyone was checking them out. It was not unheard of for those with access to motor-vehicle computer records to help out criminals who might be looking to follow someone.

As scary as it sounds, the situation was under control. C.I. was back in Rikers. Before wiring him up to snag Demicco, we checked prison records to see who else was visiting this killer.

He had had two recent visitors who had convictions for witness tampering and witness intimidation. Demicco was deadly serious, and when I heard that, I thanked my lucky stars for pros like George, who insisted on taking even the slightest threat seriously.

It was summer, which created a problem wiring C.I. because inmates wore shorts in the heat and humidity of the city's island prison, making it difficult to hide the recording equipment. But this was George's specialty, and within days of returning to Rikers, C.I. was able to approach Demicco with the recorder strapped high on his inner thigh.

When we heard the conversation on tape, we were relieved, disappointed, and surprised! We heard Demicco tell C.I. he was no longer interested in carrying out the hit. He said he was going upstate and did not need any more trouble.

Thus, relief, my life was apparently safe for the time being. But my team was disappointed. We had responded professionally and carefully. It would have been satisfying to bring further charges against Demicco. No one should feel they could threaten a prosecutor and get away with it. I would have liked Demicco to know we were onto him, but we could not expose C.I.

But I was grateful to him because he earned his keep. Showing a real flair for the undercover life, he had the presence of mind to ask Demicco exactly why he wanted me to die.

The mobster's answer was the surprise that still boggles my mind: "Are you kidding? That louse disrespected me. You know what he did? He had that little girl do the sentencing. I'm a made man," he boasted, "and he had a little girl send me away. Fuck him!"

George and I looked at each other in amazement. How do you figure on something like that? I laughed a nervous laugh. It was so unpredictable. I was going to die because I let a young female assistant stand up in court against a wiseguy! Go figure that one out.

I thought I knew the rules of the street as well as the rules of the courtroom, but there's always something to learn in the courtrooms of Brooklyn. Over the years I realized how lucky we were that Demicco did not decide to take it out on Karen.

Chapter 2

Two Murdered Cops

Success is not final, failure is not total; it is the courage to continue that counts.

—Winston Churchill

I had been threatened before and would be again.

The one time that bothers me to this day followed one of the most emotional periods I ever had working for the District Attorney's Office. It involved a notorious member of the radical, murderous Black Liberation Army named Cleveland Davis, a figure in the Attica riots.

On April 2, 1978, the day my sister, Pamela, was married, two police officers from the Seventy-Ninth Precinct were shot to death when they stopped two men they saw leave a car on a busy residential street. We'll never know why they decided to stop and question them because the two men answered their questions with gunfire. In a short gunfight, Officers Christie Masone, thirty-three, and Norman Cerullo, twenty-nine, and one of the men were killed. The second man, shot in the leg, escaped in the car he had arrived at the scene in.

That man, Cleveland "Jomo" Davis, was captured a few blocks away after he passed out from loss of blood and ran the car into a parked car. An off-duty officer named Jim Dennedy, who was rushing one of the wounded cops to the hospital in his own car, noticed the accident.

When he heard the circumstances of the shooting, he returned to the accident scene, and when a witness pointed out the injured Davis as the man who'd just shot the cops, Dennedy arrested him. Officer Paul Cirucina joined Dennedy, and they rode with Davis in the ambulance.

During the ride Davis tried to escape from the ambulance. He got Cirucina's gun and tried to shoot his way out. Dennedy was not about to let that happen. The three men struggled in the back of the speeding ambulance, and when Davis pulled the trigger, Dennedy jammed his own hand into the gun in front of the hammer, stopping it from engaging the firing pin. It took many blows to the head to finally subdue Davis, but the frantic ambulance ride ended at the emergency room.

Davis was treated for the damage done in the struggle over the gun, but he shrewdly refused to let doctors remove the bullet from his leg. In the trials that followed his arrest, prosecutors had to rely on X-rays to show the bullet matched the size of a bullet fired by the dead police officers, but could not prove exactly that it was from one of their guns.

Two trials on charges Davis killed two cops ended in hung

juries as Davis's radical lawyers argued the killer was a third man, still on the loose, and turned the cops and eyewitnesses into the bad guys.

After the second hung jury, lawyer Robert Bloom argued for a dismissal of the charges. The then district attorney, Eugene Gold, was inclined to go along with Bloom, figuring if two juries refused to honestly weigh the evidence against Davis, a third would be a waste of taxpayers' money.

But, Phil Caruso, then head of the Patrolmen's Benevolent Association, convinced Gold to give it another try. Cops and prosecutors are not natural friends. Usually they are banging heads over cases. Cops think prosecutors go too easy on the criminals the cop arrest, and prosecutors think they have overcharged.

But when a cop is killed, the bond between the two law enforcement agencies is at its strongest. An attack on a police officer is an attack on society. Gold wanted justice for the two slain officers as much as Caruso did. So he relented.

At the time I was head of the Major Offense Bureau, a prestigious post. I had had nothing to do with Jomo Davis, as murder cases were always handled by the Homicide Bureau. But Gold called me to his office and asked me to take charge of the third trial.

He acknowledged the Homicide Bureau had done all it could in the first two trials and did not know what more could be done. It was suspected around the office that the first trial was fixed, that two jurors went into the tank for Davis. Because it was so long after the fact, we could not launch an investigation about possible jury tampering. We'll never know for certain whether it happened and, if so, who was responsible, but this is what I heard.

After the jury had been picked and the trial was in progress, Dennedy was on patrol one night when he was approached on the street by a man he did not know.

"Are you the Dennedy involved in that trial?" the stranger asked.

Dennedy, alert for trouble, said he was.

"Well let me tell you, you ain't getting a conviction," the man continued. "Two brothers were fixed to dump that case."

With that said, the man walked away, leaving Dennedy a little stunned. He reported the encounter to prosecutors, but there was not much to go on to prove anything. There certainly was not enough to call for a mistrial and a new jury.

It was learned from interviews with jurors after the first trial ended in a hung jury that two jurors just refused to deliberate. They stood apart from the other ten and would not partake in discussions, so a verdict could not be reached.

The second trial was harder to explain, but the defense apparently exploited the less than stellar backgrounds of the witnesses. And sometimes a jury just does not like cops.

Gold and I decided that I should take a fresh look at everything. He arranged to have Jimmy Dennedy, the detective who'd arrested Davis, and Brooklyn homicide detective Tony Martin, a veteran Brooklyn hand, assigned to me to go over every detail of the crime, step by step.

A mystery had hung over the case since before the first trial. A witness had had a good view of the shooting from her apartment window. She never got to testify because shortly before the trial began, she came down with a bad cold and fever. She developed a cold sore on her lip that was serious enough for her to seek treatment. She was admitted to a hospital and soon died there. I looked into that death immediately after getting my marching orders from Gold, but I turned up nothing that would indicate foul play connected to the trial of Cleveland Davis.

The three of us met in my office on a Saturday morning. We were itching to get going. I suggested we return to the scene of the crime. Dennedy and Martin had been there dozens of times since the shooting. They could not imagine what we might discover on this visit.

We drove out to Throop Avenue and positioned ourselves in the spot were the two officers fell after being mortally wounded. I looked around trying to imagine how it was on that spot of this mean Brooklyn sidewalk that night. Why did they stop Davis to question him? Cops can sense when something is not right. They must have seen something or felt something. Street cops have an instinct for trouble. This was not the first time that instinct was fatal.

If possible witnesses in the surrounding buildings had seen anything from their windows, were they all questioned? I pointed to all the surrounding buildings, repeating my question. Martin said, "Yes, yes, yes," and then when I pointed to a building diagonally across the street, he froze! "You know, Mike, now that you point it out, I remember we got called away for something and never got to that building."

"Well, get to it now," I responded.

While the two detectives canvassed the building, I walked around the area. I wanted to be totally familiar with the streets when I described the night of the shooting to the jury.

When I circled back, Dennedy and Martin were both smiling from ear to ear. They'd found a woman, a middle-aged businesswoman, who remembered looking out her window and seeing the whole thing. Her nephew, now in the Air Force, was standing next to her and also saw it. No one had ever asked them before. In Brooklyn, you don't get many volunteer witnesses.

So we entered the third trial with confidence. We had two new witnesses, and their backgrounds were unimpeachable. I felt totally prepared.

Over the past several months I felt I had gotten to know the families of the murdered police officers from interviewing friends and other cops and from reading all the published reports about the case and our own investigation.

But things did not turn out the way I had anticipated.

Davis's lawyer challenged the businesswoman who'd seen the whole thing from her window. He asked her if she had owned a candy store in the neighborhood.

For many years she had owned the popular business.

Then the lawyer said, as if it were a matter of fact, that she took "numbers" in the back of the store and paid off the cops to leave her alone.

There was absolutely no evidence of that and I objected vehemently. The judge sustained my objection and chastised the lawyer, but the jury heard it. And later the lawyer even attacked the credibility of the woman's nephew, who took the stand wearing his Air Force uniform.

The trial wrapped up on a Friday, and the jury was sequestered while they deliberated. Later in the day, I was in the courtroom with Dennedy and Martin when the jury came in with some questions for the judge.

A court officer who was guarding the jurors came over to me and said things looked bad. He predicted an acquittal. Court officers shepherd jurors from the courthouse to restaurants and, if they are sequestered, to their hotel rooms at night. They hear jurors talk, although they are instructed not to talk about a case outside the jury deliberation room, and the officers sometimes hear conversations in that guarded room as well.

The next morning the jurors had still not returned, and Dennedy and now Paul Cirucina and I sat in my office waiting it out. We had worked so hard, but now, with the court officer's words in our heads, we were expecting disaster.

When the call came that the jury had reached a verdict, the three of us headed over to the courthouse. In those days police officers did not take their weapons into the courtroom, but I noticed Cirucina was carrying a gun. I knew it was not his regular on-duty weapon.

I stopped him outside the courtroom door and asked him where he was going with the gun.

He said, "Mike, I just can't take it anymore. It's killing me."

I told him he better wait outside and asked a court officer to keep an eye on him. He was trembling with anger, and the verdict had not even come yet.

When it did come, it was an acquittal. Hearing that jury foreman say "not guilty" was the worst feeling I had ever experienced in a courtroom. I did not even wait for the judge to dismiss the jury. I brushed past everyone and held back tears of frustration as I went to a small room used to prepare witnesses. I sat down in the corner, and for the first time in many years, I cried like a baby. I beat myself up mentally. What did I do wrong? I even questioned myself whether Davis was the killer. The tears flowed. I realized I was crying because I had let so many people down: the families of the cops, my new friend Dennedy, the entire Patrolmen's Benevolent Association, and the law-abiding citizens of New York. I believed at the moment and believe today that a killer walked free that morning.

If I had not stopped Paul Cirucina from going into the courtroom, he would have shot Davis in his chair before he had the chance to realize he was a free man. There is no doubt in my mind about that.

About five years later Cleveland Davis was a suspect in a robbery in Virginia. He was on the run. Two accomplices were arrested after the incident, but Davis managed to make his way to New York.

This was after I had left the DA's office and was in private practice. One morning I got a call from a Brooklyn detective. He alerted me that Davis was seen on a subway platform at Forty-Second Street near where I had my office.

The detective reminded me that Davis was desperate and warned me to be careful. I appreciated that the detective made the call, even though it did scare me. I knew what Davis was

Chapter 3

Good to Be Back

The lion sleeps tonight.

—Solomon Linda

I rejoined the DA's office in January 1992. Returning to Brooklyn, I worked in several important spots, including chief of the Homicide Bureau, where I chaired the panel that decided if a defendant would face the death penalty. Talk about pressure. A group of the most senior prosecutors in the office would go over murder cases, then recommend to the district attorney in which of the eligible cases we should seek the death penalty. I do not oppose the death penalty, but that kind of responsibility makes you careful about how you proceed and reinforces the notion that a prosecution has to be carried out letter-perfect from beginning to end to ensure proper justice. I never waivered from that belief.

The panel I chaired recommended the death penalty about twenty-five times. Hynes, a strong opponent of the death penalty, rejected us in all but two cases. In any event the New York

State legislature had not shown an appetite for the death penalty since the early sixties, when the electric chair was last used.

But the Rackets Division was where I always wanted to be.

In Rackets, the DAs were investigators and trial attorneys. There, one could prosecute across the crime spectrum against criminals of every breed: organized crime, public corruption, homicide, money laundering, terrorism, arson, police brutality, fraud, kidnapping, hate crimes, and even sex trafficking. Rackets DAs were experts on the entire universe of criminality. If there was something they did not know, they knew how to find out.

Before I got to Rackets, I won convictions in the murder of a Hasidic girl on the Williamsburg Bridge, and then in the stabbing of an Orthodox woman whose murder almost brought the Crown Heights community to riot.

I also investigated one of our own people, a crooked assistant district attorney known as the Undertaker, because he did his dirty deeds in the basement of a funeral home. He met with what we believed were bribe payers on nights and weekends in the funeral home, illegally promising favors. Over the objections of myself and other senior staff, the district attorney allowed him to resign rather than face charges even though we caught him dead to rights. We always wondered whether it was a case of local politics interfering with justice as the Undertaker was the nephew of a community political leader.

Shortly after we wrapped up that case, District Attorney Hynes called me to his corner office suite on the nineteenth floor. Somewhat to my surprise, but pleasantly so, he told me he was more than satisfied with his decision to bring me back to the fold ten years earlier.

He said he wanted me to fill an opening but first had a question to ask. I suspected this was the Rackets Division spot as my friend Dennis Hawkins had recently retired.

Hynes got out of his chair alongside his huge desk, which was covered with pictures of his family. He rarely sat behind the desk. He stood and pointed to the building far below and across Adams Street, a wide boulevard, the Kings County Supreme Court Building. There, thousands of criminal and civil trials were conducted each year by hundreds of supreme court judges supported by thousands of civil service staff.

"Mike, do you believe there is corruption in that building?"

I did and I told him so. I told him everyone thinks there are corrupt judges and lawyers and even court clerks and uniformed officers.

"Well, Mike, that's what I wanted to hear. I am naming you chief of the Rackets Division, and I want you to pursue any lead you get that would expose corruption in that building. Are you up for that?"

Of course I was, and with that I had my dream job. I have often wondered over the years if he knew something about judicial corruption that he could not tell me at that meeting. It wouldn't matter, as I would find out more than I could ever imagine.

When I came to the Brooklyn DA right out of law school in 1973, I thought it would be my home forever. I wanted to be one of the good guys. But after marriage and two children I needed to make more money, and I thought I wanted to be part of a bigger picture, to expand my horizons. So I first left to join the police department's advocate office, where I prosecuted cops who were up on departmental charges.

This important job gave me some public exposure, which I enjoyed. It also revealed the underbelly of the police department. I saw firsthand that some police officers could not be trusted and were as corrupt as some of the people they arrested. Sometimes these cops would escape criminal prosecution, but not the department's own internal affairs unit.

On the other hand, some, I learned, were victims of the byzantine politics of police headquarters. Let's face it: that system was known as a kangaroo court for good reason. But I was proud of the work I did there. We were able to weed out the bad, and I tried hard to correct any injustices brought on by the department's politicians.

Phil Caruso, the head of the Patrolmen's Benevolent Association, once took me aside at a police function to say he appreciated my work. Being that I prosecuted his members, I took that as a great compliment.

But that job also did not pay much, especially in comparison to the big bucks some of my law school classmates were making, who were also getting big headlines (which led to bigger bucks) defending the city's prominent criminals. With a wife and two sons and a mortgage and an admitted liking for expensive suits and good meals in good restaurants, the money held an attraction for me.

And I liked being among the high-powered New York elite.

I enjoyed being sought out by reporters for my thoughts on high-profile cases, even if the cases were not mine. I thrived on the action, the adrenaline pumping when a jury walked into the courtroom, and I truly believed I was saving the lives of some innocent defendants.

I had high-profile cases as a defense attorney as well. At one time I represented the actor Tony Danza of *Taxi* fame. Danza, an affable guy, was a former professional boxer. His rough speech and ability to defend himself disguised a smart mind and a nice disposition. He was working the New York Auto Show and buddying around with a bunch of New York guys when I met him.

They did a lot of drinking at the show and then even more at the bar at the Mayflower Hotel on Central Park West in Manhattan where a lot of Hollywood producers and actors stayed. At the bar they got into a juvenile food fight, which got the attention of the hotel security team. Tony told me that one of the security guys made a move to his waist, and Tony thought he was going for a gun so he coldcocked him. Tony was arrested for felony assault.

Danza reached out to the famous detective Ed Zigo, the man who arrested Son of Sam, and who was a family friend. Zigo was also a friend of mine, so he made the connection for me to represent the star.

I argued that the security guard was not badly injured and that Danza feared for his own life. The argument convinced the Manhattan district attorney to reduce the charges to a misdemeanor, and Danza was sentenced to community service.

He served his time by working as the entertainment director in an old-age home, an experience that he said made him a better person.

Danza was grateful to me and we became pals and socialized together for a while. He even invited me to his wedding, which was held at the Malibu estate of the producer Jerry Weintraub. I sat at a table right next to the entire *Taxi* cast. They were all so friendly and nice toward me. I enjoyed rubbing elbows with the Hollywood types back in New York as well, but I cannot deny it created some pressures on the home front.

Some of the people I represented were, of course, actually innocent or maybe being railroaded, such as Cibella Borges, whom the police department was trying to fire because she had posed for pictures in a slimy magazine before she became a cop. The police brass wanted her gone, and having had much experience in the department's kangaroo court, I prepared an appeal before we even heard its decision.

The police department fired her. They were outraged over the pictures. But her appeals lawyer used my papers and she won in supreme court, got her job back, and went on to be a distinguished police officer and sergeant.

But too often I knew my clients were not worth saving. The prosecution was mandated to bring its strongest case against them, whether for homicide or grand larceny or pickpocketing. My job under the ethical standards of the profession I loved with all my heart was to argue against that prosecution with the strongest case I could present. I was good at it. I knew how to handle a jury, my openings and closing summations brought me the attention of law professors. But sometimes I questioned w. I was doing. Sometimes an acquittal for my client would be returned by the jury and I would say to myself, "This guy belongs in jail."

And the money did not turn out to be what I had been expecting. I wasn't able to do for my family what I had hoped. In addition, I often had to fight to get paid, especially if I lost a case. Try to get $50,000 from a guy who was just sentenced to fifteen years in jail. Good luck!

In one case, I overcame great odds to win and still couldn't get paid. Two dimwits had been passengers in a friend's car when it was stopped by police, who suspected the friend of being a drug dealer. My clients were sitting in the back, the suspect was driving, and another man was in the front. When police searched the car, they found two huge bags of heroin under the backseat. Everyone in the car was arrested, charged with A1 felony possession. Conviction could mean life in prison even though my clients had never been convicted of anything before.

The two were referred to me. I interviewed them and decided they were dumb but not heroin dealers. I believed they did not know the drugs were in the car. I convinced a jury of that, and the two walked free. And they acted like their legal defense was free. I saved them from life behind bars and they stiffed me. They refused several demands for payment.

They were working as gravediggers, supporting their families and living decent lives, not rotting away in Attica. Finally I had to sue them in civil court, where an order to garnish their wages was issued. That took me more than a year to accomplish.

They each owed me $10,000, which I eventually recouped from their paychecks.

I had even done a little political campaigning for Mayor Ed Koch in his run against Mario Cuomo for governor in 1982. Working on campaigns is a good way for lawyers to make contacts that will lead to more business and maybe some government contracts, or even a senior-level job in a government agency, if your candidate wins. Koch lost that race.

So, truth be told, after many hours of introspection, I realized I was not happy with my life as a defense attorney, and when District Attorney Hynes asked me to return to the fold in 1991, I jumped at the chance.

My dream to someday become Rackets chief ignited when I was around eighteen years old. I was in my second year of college and I had begun dating my now ex-wife. Both of us were at St. John's. We met the year before while she was pledging her sorority and I was pledging my fraternity. As things started to get serious in the next couple of years, I met her family.

She was living in lower Manhattan with her mom and sister. Her dad, an NYPD detective, had died years before, and she had a number of aunts, uncles, and cousins to whom she was close. She came from a family of cops. One of her uncles, Jimmy, was a first-grade NYPD detective who worked at the Brooklyn DA's office under District Attorney Eugene Gold. Jimmy was a highly regarded and highly decorated detective and a recognized fingerprint expert, who, during the hunt for the serial killer David Berkowitz, known as Son of Sam, was tapped to work on fingerprints recovered from the various crime scenes. When I met him, he had been on the police force for more than thirty years.

I got to know Uncle Jimmy well. Everybody in the family knew that I had my heart set on going to law school, and because of that Jimmy took it upon himself to get me interested in a career in the DA's office. I would spend hours with him on visits to his apartment in Manhattan and to his home on the Jersey Shore. Like many cops he was a colorful storyteller. I listened with delight to stories of his exploits in the NYPD.

During his years in a detective squad he was assigned to precincts in south Brooklyn, which was home to many mobsters, and he spent a good amount of time on mob investigations. I found the organized-crime, or Mafia, characters fascinating and was engrossed in the *catch me if you can* stories Jimmy would tell about his pursuit of them. The more I listened to them, the more I became interested in doing that work from a prosecutor's office.

I wanted to be a good guy, the guy in the white hat on the white horse, like Jimmy and his friends.

It was perfect for me: I could combine my love for the law with the excitement of chasing mobsters. The DA's office became my goal, and being the head of the unit that did these mob investigations and prosecutions was the place I wanted to land someday.

And if the stories of the mob were not enough to pique my interest, something that had gone on in what would become my Brooklyn neighborhood clinched it for me.

During the early sixties a branch of the Colombo family had

its headquarters in Carroll Gardens. Then the family was called the Profaci family, and the faction that lived and *worked* and hung out in my neighborhood was headed by "Crazy" Joe Gallo. Gallo and his brothers, Albert "Kid Blast" Gallo and Larry Gallo, controlled the mob operations in this neighborhood, especially on the docks. I wanted to bang heads with guys like that.

They also were into gambling and loan-sharking and operated out of a social club on President Street a block away from where I once had an apartment. The head of the family, Joe Profaci, was not a favorite of the Gallo brothers, and they were not favorites of his. Their dispute at that time was over the most important commodity in the mob: money.

The Gallo boys were good earners and felt that they were not keeping enough of their earnings, that Profaci demanded too high a percentage be kicked up to him. This led to the Gallo-Profaci war.

In this shooting war bodies were dropping all over south Brooklyn. The Gallos were ruthless but outnumbered by the Profaci soldiers. Because of the number of casualties, the NYPD put together a squad of seasoned detectives to ride herd on both factions in the hope that this would discourage the shooters and end the war. The unit became known as the Pizza Squad, for obvious reasons. They were mostly Irish American detectives, and one of the prominent members was my wife's uncle Jimmy Murphy. The stories of the squad's exploits were mesmerizing, and he and I spent hours talking about them. I devoured Jimmy

Breslin's book about the war, *The Gang That Couldn't Shoot Straight.*

My uncle Jimmy had told me about one part of the book, otherwise I would not have believed it. The Gallos kept a lion in the basement of their social club! They brought enemies there and scared the shit out of them to get them to do what the Gallos wanted. According to my uncle Jimmy, it worked. What the enemies didn't know was that the lion, for all its ferocity, had no teeth!

The whole Pizza Squad thing hooked me, and when it was coupled with the other stories, I was ready to start chasing wiseguys right then and there.

When I finally got into law school, Jimmy asked me if I was interested in an internship at the Brooklyn DA's office, which of course I was. Between my first and second year in law school I did that internship, and in my mind my career was right there. This is what I wanted to do, and I eventually realized my goal: I was named chief of the Rackets Division in the Kings County District Attorney's Office by District Attorney Charles "Joe" Hynes in April 2001. I knew Uncle Jimmy, who had passed away, was smiling down on me.

Chapter 4

Death of an Angel

Angels are like diamonds. They can't be made, you have to find them. Each one is unique.

—Jaclyn Smith

About two years before Hynes gave me the Rackets Division, a young woman named Amy Watkins was stabbed to death as she fought with purse snatchers on a quiet street in Prospect Heights.

Amy was a social worker from Topeka, Kansas, who had been living with her divorced mother in St. Louis, Missouri. She moved to New York to obtain her master's degree in social work at Hunter College. On March 8, 1999, she was an intern working with battered women at the New Settlement Community Center in the Bronx. At nine forty-five that evening as she huddled against a cold wind while walking from the subway to her apartment in Prospect Heights, she stopped at a grocery store, where three men lingered outside. Minutes after she left, she was assaulted by the three men, who had followed her from the store.

They were after her purse. She screamed, a long scream, when she realized what was happening.

As she struggled to hold on to her purse and break away, one of the attackers stabbed her in the back with a twelve-inch kitchen knife with such brute force the blade passed through her body. She screamed again, this time shorter, a bloodcurdling scream for her life. As she fell to the ground, the men grabbed her purse and fled. They got away with $8.

Paramedics rushed to the scene. In a desperate effort to save her they tried but failed to pull the knife from her body. Twenty-six years old, she died in the street.

Amy's murder had all the elements of a big tabloid story and it got that attention, even though the city's media were dealing with two other major stories at the time. "The Yankee Clipper," Joe DiMaggio, New York's greatest sports hero, died earlier that morning, and that afternoon John Cardinal O'Connor, the leader of New York's Catholic community, announced he was stepping down.

But Amy's story resonated with New Yorkers, who were just getting comfortable with a shrinking murder rate and safer city. Murders had dropped consistently for the past ten years. In 1990 there were an incredible 2,605. The year Amy joined the list of victims, there were 903.

Amy was an angel on earth. She was beautiful; she actually worked part-time as a model for Pratt Institute art students. She was a loving daughter, and she was dedicating her life to helping battered women. The entire city grieved for her. Three days after her murder a few hundred New Yorkers, most of whom did not know her but were moved by news reports of the horrid crime, held a candlelight vigil for her in Prospect Heights, and Rudy Giuliani, New York's crime-fighting mayor, attended her wake.

On March 13 friends and family and fellow students and her teachers packed into the small Church of the Resurrection in Manhattan to bid her farewell. "Amy's was a life of gifts, of gifts received and gifts given. Amy multiplied those gifts and shared them on the stoop of her apartment building, in the neighborhood diner, or in the bodega near the settlement," said one of her supervisors at work. Amy had a lot of friends; one of them eventually became a social worker in the District Attorney's Office.

A woman who was a member of the domestic-violence survivors group that Amy oversaw marched in the vigil with her daughter. She summed up the feelings of all who knew Amy. "Amy was our angel, and now God is taking her away to help other people," she told the reporters covering the march. "And now, God needed her somewhere else."

From then on Amy was remembered as an angel. She deserved the praise. One of her teachers from the Hunter College School of Social Work spoke at the service about how Amy would joke about being from Kansas, from the land of Dorothy and Toto.

Amy's grandparents, parents, her boyfriend, and a brother fought to hold back tears during the service but lost the battle as mourners followed the coffin out the doors of the church. Her father, Lawrence, a teacher who lived in New Jersey, told the media how deeply he was moved by the outpouring of emotion from so many people who did not even know Amy. "We are very grateful to all New Yorkers for their tremendous support," he told reporters. Amy was buried in St. Louis where her mother, Margaret, lived.

The crime touched me personally as well. I grew up in Prospect Heights. I lived most of my life, until I was a college student, in a four-room apartment with my parents and sister, Pamela, on Prospect Place, just around the corner from Park Place where Amy lived years after we had moved away.

I had one of those urban childhoods that seem so desirable in the movies. My neighbors were mostly Irish with some Italians and Jewish families and a sprinkling of Hispanics and African-Americans as the years went by. In this hardworking neighborhood, blue-collar families put in long hours and vacationed for a few weeks at the Jersey Shore or in the Catskills or by taking a road trip to Florida. It was the picture of middle-class prosperity. Most crimes were not felonies and were adjudicated by the beat cop and your father. My friends grew up to be cops, firefighters, and sanitation workers, with an occasional lawyer, doctor, or academic like my sister thrown in. It was similar to many New York neighborhoods in all the boroughs through the 1960s.

But drugs and a struggling economy took their toll in Prospect Heights as they did everywhere else as the city fell into two decades of deterioration. Those who could afford to moved to the suburbs, mostly Long Island. Crime rates soared and the crimes became more serious. The growth was in the types of crimes that scared people the most: random muggings, rapes, home invasions, mostly fueled by the scourge of crack. The symbols of the city became graffiti-covered subway cars and squeegee men who terrorized tourists.

Things started turning around in the late eighties, and by the time Amy Watkins arrived from St. Louis, Prospect Heights was regaining its old flavor as a safe, middle-class, now gentrifying neighborhood. I even entertained thoughts of moving my family back there.

So when the news of Amy's murder was reported to me, it struck home like no other crime I had dealt with in my career.

I was chief of trials, in charge of the five bureaus that tried cases of all types, assigned by the geographic area each bureau covered. The bureaus had their own chiefs as well, but all reported to me.

This was the busiest division of the office, handling about two hundred trials a year and dealing with about a thousand indictments. The division was staffed by young, relatively new assistant district attorneys, supported by a cadre of experienced veterans who kept the wheels turning. I liked the assignment because there was never a dull moment.

Walk through the Supreme Court Building at any time of day and you would find prosecutors from the Trial bureaus hammering out plea deals, examining witnesses, addressing a jury, or awaiting verdicts. Their work was sometimes underappreciated, but I believed they were the foundation of the District Attorney's Office.

I figured Amy's case would go to the Homicide Bureau, but

I wanted to be involved in it. I felt I owed it to my old neighborhood, to the memories of the people who lived there and worked to make it a safe, happy place for me to grow up.

That's why I took that murder so personally.

There were no suspects immediately after the attack. It looked like it would be a long, drawn-out process before the police nailed down anyone for the crime, even with the pressure coming from City Hall.

I went to the district attorney and asked if I could prosecute the killers when they were apprehended. I knew that other prosecutors could do a good job; we had an agency bursting to the seams with highly competent lawyers. But I was burning with an inner rage over this. I have no rational way to explain it. I just felt I needed to do it, like I was destined to do it.

Hynes wondered why I was so interested, and I told him about my attachment to the neighborhood. I told him about my love for the people who lived there when I was growing up.

Hynes grew up in Flatbush, son of a working mother, and still lived there with his wife, Pat, and their children. He understood what I felt. He told me that it would be my case and suggested I let the Homicide Bureau chief, Barry Schreiber, know. I thought Barry's nose would be a little out of joint. He was no shrinking violet and this would be a high-profile case. But he also understood my desire. He readily agreed to let me take the case.

One week after the murder it appeared we were in for the long haul as the NYPD detectives were telling us there still were no legitimate suspects. It was now my responsibility to seek justice for Amy Watkins, so I put it on my schedule to stay in touch with any progress the detectives might be making and got on with my work running the Trial Division.

The city put up an $11,000 reward for information leading to the conviction of the killer or killers. Detectives put together a sketch of a suspect with information provided by a man who said he was around the corner from the scene of the attack and ran into a guy hurrying past him toward Prospect Park. He described the man as Hispanic, wearing a dark jogging suit. The sketch led nowhere.

Weeks and months passed with no strong leads developed by the police, and the case eventually faded from the headlines. But it was always on my mind. I checked in regularly with the Brooklyn homicide detectives who were assigned to catch the killer. I became a thorn in their side. If they told me about a lead they had followed, I questioned every move they made. After a while they did not want to take my calls. But I wanted this killer caught. I wanted to put the man who ran a twelve-inch knife through the back of Amy Watkins behind bars for life.

In August 2000, I was eating lunch at my desk when Barry Schreiber stuck his head in. "Mike, the cops have a woman, arrested for drugs, facing heavy time, who gave them a lead on the Watkins case. They have three guys at the Seven-Seven they like as the killers. Do you want to go over there?"

Boy, I had been waiting for that call for more than a year. You bet I wanted to go over there. Barry said he would go as well to take the statements. You try not to have the prosecutor who will be trying the case take the initial statements from suspects to avoid their becoming witnesses in the trial. Schreiber also grabbed Jon Besunder, deputy chief of the Homicide Bureau, and we rushed to the Seventy-Seventh Precinct on Utica Avenue.

My adrenaline was pumping as we raced to the precinct. I thanked Barry for remembering I requested the case. In my mind I went over the details as I remembered them. Midevening, she was coming home from her intern position in the Bronx, she struggled with the killer, twelve-inch knife plunged through her body. Two screams, one horrific. Dead at the scene. Newspapers calling her an "angel."

It all came back to me as I entered the squad room on the second floor of the precinct to face the suspects. The detectives told us what had led up to the arrests. A crack addict under arrest was trying to make a deal with them. As a confidential informant she provided the names of David Jamison, Felix Rodriguez, and Pierre Antoine as the purse-snatching team that ambushed Amy Watkins and left her dead a few blocks from her home.

The three suspects were all in custody when we arrived at the precinct. By that time detectives had taken statements from all three. First, Jamison and Rodriguez made oral statements to the detectives, then they wrote out statements in their own hand. They offered what amounted to confessions. The third, Pierre Antoine, said he had nothing to do with the crime. Now we were here to listen to their statements once again and videotape them.

A technician from the DA's office arrived and set up his camera in the captain's small office on the second floor. Schreiber,

Besunder, and Detective John Barba went in to continue the interrogation of Jamison. They would get it on videotape. They left the door open and I stood just outside where I could hear every word.

For the third time Jamison told how the trio had spotted Amy in the grocery store and thought her an easy mark. They followed her for about half a block, then Jamison admitted to rushing up behind her with the knife. He said Rodriguez went through her coat pockets, then Jamison and Antoine grabbed her purse. But Amy fought back, and Jamison said she backed into the knife he was holding. He said he did not intend to kill her. As he saw it, it was her own fault she was stabbed to death.

Jamison said the three men then separated and fled. He said he cut off his dreadlocks because news accounts reported there were witnesses, and he ran to Pennsylvania to wait until things cooled down. (He had no idea the news accounts were not exactly correct.) Months later, when he felt it was safe, he returned to the Brooklyn apartment that he shared with his wife and their young child. The mother and child were waiting just down the hall when Jamison gave his account, a fact that would loom large in the trial.

Rodriguez, twenty-one, gave a similar account, admitting he grabbed the purse but denying he knew anything about a knife until he saw Jamison stab Amy.

Antoine denied being there completely. He said he did not know anything about it.

Based on their statements, Schreiber okayed the arrests on murder charges of Jamison and Rodriguez, but had to cut Antoine loose because all we had were the uncorroborated statements of the codefendants. Under New York law, that was not enough to support an arrest. I knew right then that we did not have a strong case. Outside of the statements we had nothing to tie them to the crime. All we had were two suspects blaming each other; a witness who saw a man he described as Hispanic run past him on the street; a woman who saw a black man drop a purse as he ran away from the scene of the crime; and a brain-fried addict trying to avoid serious drug charges saying Jamison once confessed to her that he killed Amy.

Schreiber and I agreed Jamison's statement was strong and his excuse that Amy backed into the knife was absurd considering the force it would take to drive it through her body. That may sound like a lot, but it left a lot of room for a defense attorney to punch holes in our case.

For the time being though, we had two of our killers. Antoine, the best suspect for the third man, would escape prosecution unless we found a better way to connect him to the crime than snitching codefendants. That's the law.

We charged Jamison and Rodriguez with murder one, felony murder. They killed Amy Watkins while assaulting her to steal her purse. They would face life in prison without parole.

By the time we left the precinct that evening the news had spread throughout the city that the killers of the "angel" were in custody. We hoped the news would bring out some more witnesses, maybe some people who were afraid to come forward while the killers were still on the loose. The media can be useful that way.

That is one purpose served when suspects are paraded in front of news cameras as they are taken from the station house to court. It's called a perp walk. *Perp* is short for "perpetrator." It is not unusual for witnesses of a crime to recognize a suspect they see on television or in the newspapers. If they come forward, they can often make a weak case much stronger.

About ten years earlier I'd prosecuted a cop named Robert Cabeza, who, while off duty, robbed a liquor store in Bedford-Stuyvesant. He and an accomplice, with another man keeping lookout, went in a little after midnight. Cabeza, who was in civilian clothes, flashed his police badge and asked to use the bathroom. The storeowner gave him the okay, and the off-duty cop went behind the glass-protected counter. He then drew his gun and demanded the owner and a clerk empty the cash register.

The two frightened men complied, but Cabeza said, "They saw my face, they gotta go," and he and the accomplice shot them anyway. The owner died.

The store was just around the corner from the cop's apartment, and as he fled, he was recognized by a few neighborhood residents. But before he was caught for the liquor-store murder-robbery, he staged another robbery, this time in an upscale restaurant on Madison Avenue in Manhattan.

The night he was arrested for the murder, police perp-walked him from in front of the precinct to a car that would take him to court in full view of the news media. The next day the police department received calls from people who said they recognized the killer cop as the man who robbed them in the Madison Avenue restaurant. In addition to robbing the owner's cash register, Cabeza had then robbed each patron. Eleven of them recognized him in the perp-walk pictures on television and in the newspapers and identified him in court.

After I convicted Cabeza of felony murder and the accomplice of robbery in the first degree, Cabeza was transferred to Manhattan, where he was found guilty of the Madison Avenue holdup. The judge sentenced him to eleven consecutive terms of twenty-five years each for that caper.

So sometimes the media get in the way of an investigation, but sometimes they serve a useful purpose.

Jamison and Rodriguez were both held without bail. The trial of Jamison, the man with the knife, would come first. The court appointed the smart, competent Sam Gregory as his lawyer because Jamison could not afford to hire one.

Schreiber assigned Assistant District Attorney Kyle Reeves to assist me, second seat as it is known. A good second seat is crucial to any prosecution. He could give the opening or closing argument, although I usually kept the closing for myself, and could examine some of the witnesses, such as technical or medical experts as the trial progressed.

Of course the district attorney would want regular updates. This was a high-profile case. The murder of an idealistic young social worker who came to New York to help people in need made national headlines. Her random killing made the city appear unsafe. Probably hundreds of fathers across the country, maybe the world, talked their daughters out of moving to New York after they heard about Amy's fate.

It was up to me to make sure that while bad things happen, this city would not tolerate them. The devil would be brought to justice in Brooklyn. That's the way I looked at it.

As is typical of those days in Brooklyn, the case took almost eighteen months to wind its way to the trial date. In the meantime, early in 2001, I was appointed chief of the Rackets Division by DA Hynes. I had achieved my goal. It was the spot I had always wanted.

I was replacing my good friend Dennis Hawkins, who had recommended me for the job to Hynes. Dennis was leaving because he was fed up with a lot of the bullshit that comes with working in a bureaucracy as large as the Brooklyn District Attorney's Office. He and I had become friends when we worked together on the Undertaker case. A bond between us formed around Hynes's regular meetings with office executives. Hynes was always interested in new ideas to attack the growing crime rates, and he had a special interest in reducing recidivism, which he saw as the most effective way to bring down crime.

Dennis and I would roll our eyes at some of the suggestions made by the kind of sycophants who knew how to rise in a bureaucracy without ever having actually accomplished anything such as major convictions or having groundbreaking new ideas. We were both disappointed by how much Hynes was influenced by those snide gossipmongers and rumor spreaders who had no record of achievement or ever offered worthwhile ideas.

Dennis had a track record as a prosecutor and was full of good ideas. He went on to be executive director of the Fund for

Modern Courts, a think tank, when he left our office. We've stayed close ever since.

Hynes sent Dennis; Mary Hughes, chief of the Crime Prevention Division; Joan Gabbidon, another experienced executive; and me to Boston to look at a recidivism-reduction program called the Boston Plan, which included resources from all local law enforcement agencies. We were all impressed with Boston's results. When we returned, Dennis and I met with Hynes and urged him to start a similar program. Dennis came up with a name for it, Community and Law Enforcement Resources Together; it would be known as ComAlert. It was all about assisting convicts who were returning to their communities and teaching them the skills they would need to readjust to society and to help them avoid the pitfalls that would return them to prison.

The program taught classes in basic academic and vocational skills and helped find jobs for enrollees. It resulted in dramatically lower recidivism rates for those who were in the program as compared to former convicts who did not have such a program available to them. It was one of the most successful programs Hynes ever developed, and Dennis, Mary Hughes, and I were most responsible for bringing it to Brooklyn.

I took over a Rackets Division that was involved in a wide range of investigations, worked by prosecutors who were equal parts detectives and trial attorneys. This is what I wanted. I was eager to get going.

Dennis's office had been on the nineteenth floor, the executive floor, as was mine as chief of trials. My first move was to relocate downstairs to a new office on the seventeenth floor of the two-year-old building on Jay Street where the entire District Attorney's Office had moved as part of the renaissance of downtown Brooklyn. I wanted the staff to think of me as one of them, someone who would be just a few feet away with an open-door policy. I wanted them to see how hard I worked and follow my lead.

I took my notes on Amy's case with me. That was my case, and I would stick with it to the end no matter what my position in the office would be.

As the trial date approached in May, I suggested to many of my new staff they come to the courtroom to see me in action. I wanted them to know that they had an experienced, knowledgeable, dynamic prosecutor as their new head. I was proud of my record in the courtroom and saw no reason to be shy about it. I knew young prosecutors could learn something from the way I prepared a case and conducted myself in court. I was not intimidated by hotshot defense attorneys or pedantic judges who looked down their noses at young assistants. I relished the legal arguments and knew how hard I could push without jeopardizing my cases.

About two months prior to the trial date I began prepping my witnesses. My main evidence was going to be Jamison's own videotaped statement. He gave himself up pretty neatly. But his lawyer, Sam Gregory, had an ace in the hole I would eventually have to deal with.

As for human witnesses, the pickings were slim. I would put

the EMTs who tried to save Amy on the stand, as well as Detective Barba, who would describe how he got to the purse snatchers and obtained Jamison's confession. The man who found her body on the street also would testify. And I would put the medical examiner on the stand, who would describe the horrific fatal wound, making the defense that Amy backed into the knife sound incredible. But my star witness would be her father, Lawrence Watkins.

Leading up to the trial, I got to know Mr. Watkins well. He was an impressive man, someone I grew to admire.

My experience had been that parents of victims are often blinded by their desire for vindication. They are looking for ways to strike back at the defendant. Barring any physical attempt to harm them, their only opportunity may come when they get a chance to testify. That's when they can portray the difference between their child and the person who killed him or her.

These witnesses have to be handled with kid gloves. In questioning them you do not want to cross the line, and elicit answers so filled with anger and vitriol that they will seem irrational. The last thing you want the jury to believe is that the child may have behaved like the parent, somehow contributing to the horrific actions that took the child's life.

I did not have to worry about that with Lawrence Watkins. A gentle man, he weighed his words and actions carefully. He did not push me to *get the defendant at all costs*. He understood we had Jamison dead to rights, but also understood things could go wrong in a trial. He did not want to throw a wrench in the works. He told me he just wanted to honor Amy's memory.

He asked me what would happen if he broke down on the stand, became overwhelmed by his grief, and incomprehensible to the jury. I would have welcomed that, but I did not tell him so. His purpose on the stand was to relate the horrifying experience he had when he went to the morgue to identify Amy's body and to describe the life of Amy Watkins, the angel who was taken from us by a heinous, soulless monster named David Jamison. What juror would blame him for losing his composure. What could make him more sympathetic?

I told him what I tell all witnesses in his situation. I said I can make no promises as to how a trial will turn out. The only thing I could promise was my best effort to bring justice for Amy.

On the stand, his demeanor was perfect. He was composed and soft-spoken as he delivered heartrending testimony that made us all cry for Amy.

An incredible relationship born of a shared sense of loss developed between Lawrence Watkins and his wife, Gayle, Amy's stepmother, and Jamison's parents, James and Margo, following the arrests of Jamison and Rodriguez. They were brought together by their Christian faith and sorrow over their lost children.

The trials of Jamison and Rodriguez drew national news coverage, and an Associated Press reporter described how at the arraignment of their son in August 2000, the Jamisons felt compelled to approach Lawrence Watkins and offer their condolences. While maintaining a belief in their son's innocence, they were still able to share the grief of the Watkins family and pray for Amy as well as their own son. Margo Jamison told the AP that they were apprehensive about how the Watkins couple would react, but it turned into a "precious moment between parents."

Shortly before the trial began in May 2001, Margo Jamison suffered another loss. She was at her job as an administrative worker at Coney Island Hospital when she went to the morgue to do the paperwork on an unidentified body that had just been brought in. The body was that of her husband, James. He had died of a heart attack on his way to work that morning.

At the trial when she told the Watkinses about her loss, they reached out to her emotionally.

"There's been some unity in our faith," Lawrence Watkins told the AP. "My wife has even said that in some sense, because of our unity as Christians, Margo and David are a part of our family."

As to David's guilt, both families understood that was in the hands of the court. It was up to me to prove the case. It was up to the defense to argue against it, and it was up to all of us to make sure Jamison and Rodriguez got fair trials. If I did not live up to my responsibility, the jury would acquit.

I relished the feeling that it was on my shoulders. When I played ball as a kid, I wanted to carry the ball. I wanted to be in the game. I wanted to be on center stage. Some have faulted me for that attitude. They say it clouds my judgment, makes me a grandstander. I say it makes me a better prosecutor, a defender of the victim, a protector of society. If that sounds corny or phony, so be it. Bring on the bad guys.

Jamison's confession was damning. First he told it to Barba.

Then he wrote it down. He repeated it to Schreiber while the technician from the DA's office videotaped it. And finally, Barba typed it all out on a police department report.

Jamison described how he, Rodriguez, and Pierre spotted Amy in the grocery store and how they followed her when she left. He said how Rodriguez and Pierre got out in front of her and he stayed behind. Their job was to stop her and grab the purse. His job was to make sure she did not resist.

During the trial, when I played the videotape of Jamison's statement in the precinct captain's office, a scream could be heard over his talking. It was coming from the street outside the open window. This was the bump in the road that I was most concerned about.

When Sam Gregory cross-examined Detective Barba, he zeroed in on that scream. Gregory said it was coming from down the hall, from the interview room where Jamison's toddler son and the boy's mother were waiting for him.

Gregory tried to make the case that Jamison was being coerced into confessing. He was made to fear his child was being hurt and only Jamison's confession could save him. It sounds absurd, but I could not laugh it off.

I addressed the issue directly and quickly in my summation to the jury. Less than a minute in I played the videotape of Jamison's confession one more time.

I told the jury to look for what was not there: "Mr. Gregory makes a big deal about this noise . . . that the scream is a baby's scream or a child's scream. I want you to listen for it, and I want you to watch the entire episode.

"I want you to watch for it, and I want you to then look and to watch for what's not there . . . Jamison does not react. Jamison does not flinch. Jamison does not do anything when that noise occurs. And they want you to believe that noise plays a role in his giving that statement, that confession, to the detectives and to Barry Schreiber.

"After you carefully watch and listen, you tell me . . . more importantly, tell yourselves when you go into that jury room, whether or not you buy the defendant's argument that he was coerced, that he was rehearsed, that he was coached, and that he was fed the story that you're about to see on this tape."

After they watched the tape, I asked them if Jamison appeared to have been threatened. "He was on videotape with an assistant district attorney. You saw it. He had a perfect opportunity to let anyone and everyone know that he had been mistreated, if in fact he had been mistreated. He had the perfect opportunity to let everyone know or anyone know that he had been intimidated or forced into the confession that you just saw.

"Jamison could have said anything at that time. But what he said was that he killed Amy Watkins, with that ridiculous excuse about her backing up into the knife." In his statement Jamison couldn't say that he drove that huge knife into Amy's back because to admit that would clearly prove an intent to kill.

After the tape played, I reminded the jurors that another detective had testified that the window in the interview room was open and below it was busy Utica Avenue in the middle of the summer, a street where kids play and babies scream as a matter of course. If it was a baby's scream, and there was no evidence it was, it came from there. It did not come from Jamison's child down the hall.

Jamison thought he was helping himself when he confessed. He minimized his role. But he was not as clever as he thought. His own description of selecting Amy as a target, following her, planning the attack, taking out the knife he was carrying—all that described the condition for felony murder, murder one, life without parole. He should have called a lawyer before he confessed. But maybe he had an attack of conscience—that's why they call it confession.

The toughest part of the summation for me was when I described Amy's screams. With her family and friends sitting in the gallery, I recounted the testimony of two witnesses who heard two screams.

"The first scream was the longer scream . . . and that's what she did when she was surprised by the people coming up and taking her bag.

"The second scream was the shorter of the two, and it came . . . when Jamison put this knife into her back, because when he did it, he killed her. That's why the second scream was shorter but more horrific than the first."

Those words sent a chill through the courtroom. Everyone sat in silence as I let the words sink in on the jury. Summations are theatrical events. It is your last chance to address the jury. You have to go for the jugular. You have to win the jury over emotionally, especially when the physical evidence is thin, as it was in this case. There was a videotaped confession, but

Gregory had thrown some shadow of doubt on it. I had to overcome that.

I knew my words would cause discomfort among the family and friends. They caused me some discomfort. But a murder trial is a blood sport. No holds barred. I knew Mr. Watkins understood that.

To wrap things up, I held two pictures of Amy. In my right hand I held a portrait taken by a friend, showing Amy looking radiant, happy, smiling. It was a picture of a young woman about to conquer the world.

In my left hand I held a picture of Amy Watkins's body taken by the medical examiner. It showed Amy laid out on a slab in the morgue. She was lying on her side with a wide, ferocious wound clearly visible in her back.

"Make no mistake, ladies and gentlemen," I said to the jury, "the evidence proves beyond a reasonable doubt that on a cold, midwinter night, on Park Place, David Jamison brutally murdered Amy Watkins. And in doing so, he turned this"—I pushed my right hand forward, showing the picture of Amy in the prime of life—"into this." I pushed the morgue photo in my left hand forward.

It was a powerful closing but I continued with a little more. I wanted to remind them of the suffering of the Watkins family. I recounted that her father waited seventeen months after the murder of his daughter until the police arrested Jamison.

"But as we all know," I said, "an arrest would not bring Amy back so that he could be at her graduation or walk her down the aisle or be handed his grandchild from Amy. Amy's memory deserves nothing less than justice be done. Do what's right, convict David Jamison of the killing, the brutal, horrible, senseless killing of Amy Watkins."

The jury deliberated for two days. Five times they emerged from the jury room to ask Judge Michael R. Juviler to explain the difference between first- and second-degree murder and the difference between stabbing with intent to kill and intent to silence.

A prosecutor does not usually like to hear the jury asking for explanations of the most serious charges because the jurors may be wavering about guilt. In this case, first-degree murder carried a sentence of life without parole, and second-degree murder carried a sentence of twenty-five years to life. Anything less than second degree here would be a defeat for the prosecution.

The jurors themselves seemed to be anxious about performing their duty. They had asked the judge to prohibit their names from being released to the public for fear of retaliation by Jamison's friends, and during the trial they twice asked for two spectators to be removed because of their threatening stares in the direction of the jury box. I could not imagine there were Jamison supporters among the spectators. But there were.

On Friday afternoon, May 18, 2001, the jury returned its verdict. Jamison was found guilty of murder in the second degree. The jurors discounted the higher count of murder one. That slightly disappointed me, but maybe we had been overreaching.

When a dramatic trial like this ends, the friends, family, media, cops, and attorneys in the gallery usually watch the convicted man being led away to the holding cells adjacent to the courtroom. Then the room quickly empties.

Kyle Reeves and I congratulated each other and gathered our notes. Then we turned to leave. As usual, a group of our colleagues were gathered in the gallery to offer congratulations, and standing there waiting for me was Mr. Watkins.

He met me as I walked past the velvet rope that separates the courtroom personnel from the gallery. I expected a handshake, but instead he wrapped his arms around me in a powerful hug.

Tears were in his eyes and he was struggling for composure. "Thank you for bringing honor to my daughter's memory."

I told him he was welcome. I told him it was my honor to serve her and her wonderful family. I offered that if I could ever do anything for them, he should not hesitate to ask.

That hug and his words are what prosecutors live for. We are not in it for the money, we are not in it because we enjoy working long, often thankless hours. We are in it to do for victims and the families of victims what they cannot do for themselves. We are in it to see that justice is done. Moments like that one with Mr. Watkins make my job the best in the world.

Outside the courtroom, I praised the jury to the press: "This jury was very careful in their analysis of the evidence. They obviously decided he was the man who did it, and they came back with the verdict they thought was appropriate.

"There is no victor. I just hope the verdict brings Mr. Watkins some closure and peace."

Outside the courtroom, Mr. Watkins, surrounded by reporters, said he hoped Mrs. Jamison could find some closure: "We pray that God will be with her in the months ahead."

Despite the judge's efforts to protect the jurors from the media, *Daily News* reporter Nancie Katz was able to corral at least one alternate juror. The alternate explained that one juror felt that the prosecution did not prove its case; that without the videotape we had nothing, and the videotape was coerced. But the entire jury was bothered by Jamison's admission that he had a knife, though not the twelve-inch knife found in Amy's body. They did not believe Jamison meant to kill Amy, and that is the way they voted.

So they were bothered by the same thing that had bothered me from day one of Jamison's arrest as well. I always knew the case depended on the videotaped confession, but I also knew it was enough. Jamison was not coerced into a confession, and no one ever threatened his child. He did the murder.

In the end, a woman outside the courthouse interviewed by a *New York Times* reporter summed up our feelings best: "Someone had to pay for what happened to this woman. She was a social worker. Can you imagine how many people she could help with her life?"

About one month later, Rodriguez was tried and, after just five hours of deliberations, was convicted of second-degree murder and first-degree robbery. We did not go for first-degree murder against him because he did not have the knife. In his statement, videotaped the same night Jamison made his, he admitted in a calm, cool fashion he was the lookout for the purse-snatching trio. His attorney also argued that the confession was coerced, but it made such little sense and was so contradictory to what was evident on the tape that the argument fell flat.

In my summation, I again told the jury to look for what was not on the tape: no sign of being rehearsed, no claim of being coerced, no hesitation to describe the events of the fateful night. Rodriguez also got twenty-five to life.

The only one to escape a trial was Pierre Antoine, who was deported to his native Haiti. That bothered Amy's stepmom. She said she would not consider the case closed as long as the third man walked free. It bothers me to this day as well that we never brought a third man, Antoine or anyone else, to justice for the murder of Amy Watkins.

Chapter 5

The Sleeping Judge

We have to remember that we have to make judges out of men, and that being made judges their prejudices are not diminished and their intelligence is not increased.

—Robert Green Ingersoll

I COULD NOT POSSIBLY KNOW it at the time, but a phone call on a Sunday morning in January 2002 from the district attorney would set off a chain of events that would control my life for the next six years and result in some of the biggest cases in the history of Kings County.

I was at my father's home in Queens. My marriage had ended and I was living with my father, whose health was in decline. But he insisted on still taking the subway to work in downtown Manhattan every morning, where he worked as a jewelry enameler, a business he started after World War II. Among other things, he made official badges for law enforcement personnel, including assistant district attorneys.

Without ceremony, the DA never apologized for interrupting a quiet Sunday or weekday dinner or even a vacation. I spent many hours on the phone with him while I was sitting on the beach on a Caribbean island. Without small talk he always got right down to business. And it worked both ways. It was not unusual for him to be interrupted while vacationing in Bermuda. He was 24/7/365, and he expected his lieutenants to be the same way.

The Kings County District Attorney's Office was the largest urban prosecution agency in the country. We had more than five hundred lawyers and seven hundred support staff. Some weeks we processed one thousand arrests. The machine never stopped, not on Thanksgiving, not on Christmas, your birthday, or your vacation. I liked that part of the job. I would not have had it any other way.

That morning Hynes told me I needed to set up a meeting with a lawyer named Gary Berenholtz. His lawyer was the well-known Ron Aiello, a former administrative judge and former chief of the DA's Homicide Bureau and my first boss. "Set it up and be as discreet as you can be. Keep it away from the building or Court Street. It is about a judge taking bribes. I want you to handle it personally." That was all Hynes said. In Rackets we got those kinds of calls all the time. My rule was to take every tip seriously, but considering the source this one had a lot more gravity.

My next call was to the ever-ready George Terra, supervising detective investigator. I told him we needed a place to interview a lawyer who had explosive information for us, but we needed to keep our activities away from the legal community. The DA's reference to Court Street meant about four blocks in downtown Brooklyn adjacent to the Supreme Court Building and Borough Hall, which were packed with offices of the county's most influential lawyers, journalists, and political operatives.

So George secured a small conference room in the Marriott Hotel that was just around the corner from my office. He reserved the room in the name of a fictitious company, Romano Associates. I thought it was a little close to home, but George convinced me that if we were seen, it would look like we were all headed to the bar restaurant on the same floor, a popular breakfast and lunch spot for lawyers, judges, and politicians. I called Aiello and told him we were set for 9:30 a.m. Monday. We did not discuss details.

When I arrived at the hotel the following morning, George was settled in place at one end of the table, his tie undone. Already in the room was Terra's boss, Chief Detective Investigator Joseph Ponzi, whom I had briefed by phone Sunday night. No significant investigation took place without Chief Ponzi's involvement. He was a veteran of the office and a consummate professional, careful to dot the i's and cross the t's. Berenholtz was there with his lawyer, Aiello. Aiello was a good friend of DA Hynes's, and it dawned on me that Aiello must have initiated this whole thing with a call to the DA. To me it meant that I would be watched carefully in this case. Not only did Hynes have an interest in rooting out corruption in the courts, but now a good friend and colleague of his would be watching my every move. Such was the politics of the DA's office—not a good thing but commonplace.

Attorneys, judges, and high-ranking court officials have close relationships. Many grew up in the same neighborhoods, went to the same schools, and worked together as young lawyers. In Brooklyn they were also members of the same political party. They were overwhelmingly Democrats, and many were active in the party's business.

Aiello introduced Berenholtz around the room, and without much ado I asked him to tell us what was bothering him. I was careful not to mention that I knew he wanted to talk about bribing a judge. I did not want to prompt him in any way. This had to be done properly. Any slipup could cost us an important case.

Berenholtz was a big but low-key guy, on first impression not the type that I thought brought in million-dollar settlements. He was nervous, but like a good lawyer, he could tell a good story under pressure. And he was under pressure.

Ponzi, Terra, and I had much experience with people who became involved in a criminal enterprise, such as bribery, then got cold feet and came to us hoping to be exonerated by giving themselves up. The nature of our jobs demanded we view those who informed with great cynicism.

Berenholtz specialized in civil cases, personal injury, often involving seven-figure settlements in which he typically received one-third. In this case, his client was an infant permanently brain-damaged in an auto accident in 1998 when a driver ran a red light, slamming into the car carrying the infant. He represented the baby in supreme court in front of Judge Victor Barron and won a $4.9 million settlement. Good work for him, but not so unusual in a case when a baby is permanently injured.

Because the baby cannot speak for itself, the judge must sign off on any agreement before the case can be officially settled and the insurance company can pay money to the plaintiff. It is called an Infant Compromise Agreement (ICA).

This was a new area of expertise for me, as it would have been for most criminal lawyers, so I listened carefully, and Berenholtz did a good job of laying it out. The Infant Compromise Agreement made good sense to me. I anticipated where the story was going. He was about to make a serious charge against an important and well-respected person.

He told us the case wrapped up the previous summer, and he was attending a hearing with Barron to discuss signing the ICA. Around lunchtime, Barron called a recess and asked Berenholtz to take a walk with him.

They left the building and headed across the street near Cadman Plaza, a parklike setting in front of the imposing steps leading up to the main entrance of the Kings County Supreme Court. Barron wanted to talk about a bribe. He was doing what the gangster John Gotti became infamous for. The wiseguys call it a walk-talk. By walking along a busy street or in the bustling plaza outside Supreme Court, the object is to make it difficult for anyone to make a recording of their conversation.

Once he felt he was safe, Barron did not waste much time. He asked Berenholtz how much his end of the ICA settlement would be. The lawyer answered $1.6 million. Barron said he had some problems because of a conflict-of-interest issue that had already been resolved. Berenholtz claimed that surprised him. It was not a big issue and was ancient history in the case. Then Barron asked him for $250,000 before he would sign the papers.

The two men continued walking, and Berenholtz, fighting to hold his composure, did not resist the offer. He said he was able to talk the price down to $115,000. He said he did not think he had a choice. His main interest was to make sure the child got what was due to her.

Now about seven months later, Berenholtz was telling us he thought the judge must have been kidding. A few days after their stroll the papers were signed. Shortly after that, Berenholtz got his fee, and until the day after New Year's 2002, he heard nothing from Barron.

This bothered me. Berenholtz agreed too quickly. I thought maybe he was used to paying judges off, maybe not in cash, but other ways: gifts, dinners, booze. But for now Berenholtz was telling us he thought he had no choice. He was in the judge's backyard: the paper guaranteeing the unfortunate child a quality life was on the desk. But Berenholtz admitted that he did agree to pay—for the infant's sake.

At this point he had broken the law. The offer of a bribe or unlawful gratuity is a crime. Obviously the payment is a crime as well as the receiving. I could have arrested Berenholtz right then for agreeing to pay the bribe. But as his lawyer, Aiello, sat quietly, taking an occasional note as did Ponzi and George, we all were thinking we had a bigger fish to fry. Berenholtz was just another lawyer; Barron was a supreme court judge.

I looked over at George and Ponzi and could tell they were as hooked, and as doubting, as I was. We were cynical about Berenholtz's motive for coming forward, but the story the way he told it up to now was believable. Then it got better.

Berenholtz said that when he left the judge that day after the ICA was signed, he was feeling pretty good. All he had to do was wait for the insurance company to send him a check. He would distribute the money to the account set up for the infant and take his seven-figure fee. He convinced himself Barron was kidding. When he did not hear from the judge for a few months, he almost forgot about his illegal deal.

But that all changed on January 2, 2002, when Berenholtz got a call from Barron asking him to come down to the judge's chambers. Two days later, Berenholtz arrived, and the judge ushered him in, locking the door behind him. Berenholtz remembered the "clunk" of the lock. The sound filled him with dread because he understood why the judge wanted to see him. "It was then I realized he wasn't kidding," Berenholtz told us.

He said he took a seat in front of the judge's desk, and Barron leaned over him and whispered in his ear, "What about the money?"

Berenholtz said the exchange shook him up. He felt Barron was a dangerous, menacing character. He did not want to pay and did not want to bribe a judge, but Barron could have an impact on Berenholtz's whole career going forward. He would certainly appear in front of the judge on other cases in the future.

Barron was holding an invisible hammer over the lawyer's head. Judges hold a great deal of power over lawyers, everything from letting them go on vacation in the middle of a case to dragging their feet on a motion that could affect the life or at least the freedom of a client and shape the lawyer's reputation. Barron was using the invisible hammer as a threat of a not-so-friendly future if Berenholtz did not pay. Barron was saying, "I haven't forgotten your promise, and I won't forget if you don't pay me." As a veteran of hundreds of trials, I understood Berenholtz's dilemma. But he should have gotten up and walked away.

From Barron's chambers, he headed directly to the office of a former law partner and unloaded his tale. The former partner suggested he seek the help of Aiello, an influential Court Street player who could guide him through some course of action that would help Berenholtz extricate himself from the mess he was in.

When Berenholtz finished, we all sat silently for a few minutes. Then I broke the ice: "You're in a bad spot, Gary. You know you should have rejected him out of hand and reported him to the administrative judge immediately." We all knew that that was what Berenholtz should have done, but we also all knew how that would have fucked up his career almost as much as getting caught making a payoff. He would have become an untouchable on Court Street. Judges would have sworn secret oaths to make him pay for turning in one of their own. Of course, I thought, that is going to be the case now anyway.

I asked him if he wanted to help himself. Aiello answered for him: "That's why we're here, Mike."

After some small talk about who knew whom and how so-and-so was—the Brooklyn law community is incredibly tight-knit—the meeting broke up and we all headed our own ways. When I got back to the office, I briefed the DA on Berenholtz's story. He agreed the big fish was Barron and ordered me to come up with a plan to hook him.

In my office later the same day, I went over the possibilities with Ponzi and Terra. George was anxious to get going: "We gotta wire him up, no doubt. He has to wear a wire and he has to get the judge asking for money. That's the only thing that will work."

George was absolutely correct. I needed something to take to a jury, and Berenholtz's story on its own would not do it. A Brooklyn jury would think he was a crook who got caught with his hand in the cookie jar and concocted a story to weasel out of it and take the judge down with him. Juries generally had low opinions of lawyers, especially those who wasted time in courtrooms and wore $1,000 suits. They rarely cut a break for a lawyer who got in trouble. But hearing Barron on tape in a menacing tone demanding money would be something they could not ignore. It wasn't my job to defend Berenholtz, but I knew he would come off as a sympathetic figure, a poor schlub being bullied by an arrogant judge. Well, maybe not such a poor schlub. He did have a $1 million fee in his bank account.

The plan was simple. Berenholtz would wear a wire and take some cash to Barron's chambers. He would wait for Barron to ask for the money, then with that demand recorded, he would hand over the cash, get up, and leave. It would have been simple if *anything* is simple.

We decided that Barron would be alerted to a problem if Berenholtz brought the entire $115,000; it would just not feel right to him. After arguing Barron down to that figure, it would be natural for the lawyer to continue to try to get away with paying less. We settled on $18,000, which we took from a fund typically maintained by law enforcement agencies for just such a purpose.

As we usually did, we recorded the serial numbers of each bill we would hand over to Barron. If the judge questioned the amount, Berenholtz was instructed to say he went to the bank twice, withdrawing $9,000 each time. This was to avoid the bank's reporting to the Feds, which they were required to do on withdrawals of $10,000 or more. It was one of the ways they tried to track money laundering.

Next came the wiring. George, having been a successful undercover operator, had a great deal of experience in this area. We thought it unlikely that Barron would search Berenholtz for a wire, but we needed to be certain whatever we planted on the lawyer would be totally concealed. We asked Berenholtz to provide a jacket that he would wear that day. We told him not to expect it back because it would be part of the evidence.

The day before the meeting, Berenholtz supplied us with a beautiful blue, double-breasted blazer with gold buttons. George ran wires no thicker than a human hair through both lapels of the jacket. The wires would transmit any sound they picked up to a recorder as small as a pillbox in Berenholtz's pocket. George, displaying the skill of a Hong Kong tailor, went to work. Because we expected Barron to be whispering in Berenholtz's ear, George sliced open both lapels and ran the wires almost the length of the jacket. When he finished, it was impossible to spot that anything on the jacket had been altered in any way. We kidded him about what his next profession could be when he finally got tired of detective work.

I got no sleep the evening before the meeting. The DA called me several times to go over the plan again and again. "Are you sure this recorder will work?" he must have asked me a dozen times. All I could say was we had a pretty good track record in using hidden cameras and recorders. Terra and Ponzi knew their craft. But I understood why Hynes was so antsy. Catching a supreme court judge breaking the law was a rare event.

A year earlier Judge Jerome D. Cohen was indicted for accepting bribes in exchange for steering money from children's trust funds he controlled into a Brooklyn credit union. He was acquitted. Another Queens judge, William C. Brennan, was nailed in 1986 for taking bribes to fix criminal cases. He did twenty-six months in federal prison. In 1987, Manhattan Supreme Court judge Hortense Gabel had been indicted on federal conspiracy and mail-fraud and bribery charges. She had been acquitted. That same year, perjury charges against Queens judge Francis X. Smith for lying to a federal grand jury landed him a year in jail and tainted his otherwise great career. If things went right, we would soon be adding Victor I. Barron to this rogues' gallery. Barron was not well-known outside Brooklyn, but this case was explosive and sure to attract major media coverage because of the exploitation of an infant and of course the tape we planned to have.

As we were going over last-minute details in my office, which was a short walk from Barron's chambers, Berenholtz realized that he would not be able to walk through the court's metal detectors with the wire sewn into his lapels. Surprisingly, no one had thought of that. It would surely set off alarms. I could have called the court officers to arrange for our man to get through, but that would reveal what we had going on. Someone certainly would tip off Barron before Berenholtz got to his chambers. Simple suddenly became complicated.

Thankfully, George came up with a solution. He suggested that he and Berenholtz switch jackets. George was authorized to bypass the metal detectors by showing his ID and could wear the lawyer's jacket into the building. Berenholtz would wear George's jacket. They switched and met a few minutes later in a men's room to switch back.

At the judge's chambers, Barron held the door to let Berenholtz in, and as the lawyer passed, the judge closed it behind him and locked it. *Clunk!* Berenholtz took his customary seat in front of the judge's desk. Barron approached and asked Berenholtz how he was and wished him a happy New Year. Then he leaned over him and whispered in his ear, "You have it?" Berenholtz responded, "Here it is. Eighteen thousand dollars," to which Barron replied, "Don't make me chase you for the rest." After a little small talk, Berenholtz left.

A few minutes later, he and Aiello were in my office recounting what had occurred. Berenholtz was not the happiest guy in the world, but Ponzi, George, and I were pumped up. We let Berenholtz go but ordered him to leave the blue blazer with the wire and the recorder.

If we did not score with this tape, we would probably not get another chance. But the recording, when we played it, supported Berenholtz's version of the event. But he left something important out. Something that in my mind clinched this case more than the money would. When we listened to the tape, we heard Barron greeting Berenholtz and heard them shuffle through the door, and then, clear as day, *Clunk!* went the old door just as Berenholtz had described it in the past. A jury would eat that up, I thought. *Clunk,* the door was closing on Barron.

The three of us took the tape up to Hynes's office. The district attorney listened to the tape, congratulated us for doing a great job, and ordered us to arrest Barron the day after Martin Luther King Day, which was a few days away.

I was a bundle of nerves all weekend. Mostly, I was worried about word of the investigation being leaked to the media. While the circle of involvement was small—me, Ponzi, Terra, two detectives Terra picked for a backup team for the arrest, Aiello, Berenholtz, and Hynes himself—our office was known to leak like a sieve. Routine investigations often appeared in the media before our own press office even knew about them. Usually it did no harm, and sometimes it was even helpful, but this was not routine.

We were taking down a supreme court judge. We were 100 percent in the right, his own words were going to hang him. But Barron had his own supporters; he might have been a small player in Brooklyn politics, but he had to have some local politicians who cared about him. After all, he had to get elected to the bench, as he did in 1998, and some would defend him to the hilt, saying Berenholtz was not a Brooklyn player, his office was in Manhattan, he was a manipulative crook who set the judge up.

On Sunday the day before the holiday, Hynes reached me on my cell phone while I was watching my son Andrew play basketball. Hynes said he wanted me to be on the scene of the arrest personally. That was unusual. DAs were rarely involved in the physical act of an arrest. It indicated that Hynes was as strung out as the rest of us.

Over the holiday weekend, while the office was pretty much empty, Ponzi organized a TAC, or tactical meeting, for the arrest team. I often observed these meetings and heard the plans, but now, thanks to Hynes's orders, I was part of the operational team. We knew that Barron played tennis early every morning. We believed he would leave his house around 6:00 a.m. to go to his tennis club. We decided not to take any chances and set our stakeout to begin at 4:00 a.m. on Tuesday following the MLK holiday.

We were a little concerned because our surveillance team had not seen Barron the entire three-day weekend. We thought he might have gone away. I worried that he might have gotten wind of our investigation. I feared he was gone for good. Maybe we'd waited too long to make the pickup. Or maybe Berenholtz tipped him.

I didn't sleep at all the night before. I sat in my bedroom going over the notes we had from our meetings and replaying the Berenholtz tape in my mind. I envisioned playing the tape for a jury and imagined their response when they heard that *clunk,* the sound of the lock on the door in Barron's chambers. I knew we had the bum, but the problem that morning was getting him in cuffs and to our office as discreetly as possible.

By 5:00 a.m. George and I were sitting in his undercover car across the street from the judge's neat single-family home. The quiet block on a wide, two-way street was one of the best family neighborhoods in Brooklyn. The judge's car was parked in his driveway close to his side door.

Our backup team was about two blocks away facing the opposite direction. At 6:00 a.m. the house remained dark, with no apparent movement inside. Maybe he'd noticed us sitting across the street and was inside panicking. George, who had seen everything and never panicked, conceded he was getting nervous as well.

Around 7:00 a.m. we called the backup unit and discussed packing it in for the day. We thought we would have to head for the courthouse, maybe find him there, and, if not, put out a warrant for his arrest. In the middle of that discussion a light came on in the downstairs floor of his house. A collective sigh of relief filled the streets of Marine Park.

Within minutes he came out, dressed in his tracksuit and carrying his tennis racket. Barron at sixty was a good-looking, athletic man and kept himself fit. He backed his car out of the driveway and, as we'd predicted, headed in the direction of the backup team. George gave them the heads-up, and they let the judge drive a few blocks to near the Kings Plaza shopping center before tapping the siren and red lights on their car and ordering him to pull over.

The judge complied right way as the backup car pulled up behind him. No way did we think we were dealing with a physically dangerous criminal, but why have a backup team and not use them?

George flashed his red lights and pulled up in front of Barron, cutting him off in front, and we got out of the car. As George and I approached from the front and the other two detectives from the rear, Barron got out of his car, saying, "It's all right, guys, I'm a supreme court judge," and took a few steps toward us.

"We know that, Your Honor. We know who you are," I replied. "Please just stand still."

He stopped and said again, "I'm a supreme court judge. Everything is okay here."

George said, "You have to come with us. You're under arrest. Please get into the car."

Barron froze in place. Clearly he was trying to absorb what was happening. A police car with its red lights flashing was blocking his car, and another police car blocked the street behind him. He may have recognized me. I repeated what George had said, "You have to come with us." I had never been involved in anything like this before, and I hoped I was not screwing up or acting like a novice. I was nervous but confident I was not showing it.

God only knows what was going through Barron's mind. Was he thinking of Berenholtz, or was he thinking of some other crime he might have committed? He did not say a word. George held the door for him, we did not handcuff him, and speechless and clearly stunned, he got into the back of George's car. George got in front and I went around and got in back with Barron.

The backup team took Barron's car and we all headed to our office on Jay Street. George and I were quiet. There was nothing to say. What we had just done would be rocking the criminal justice system of not only Brooklyn but New York State by the end of the day. This was why I loved the Rackets Division. This was important. It was different. This was the kind of thing we did. After a few blocks, I looked over at the judge. He was sitting up straight, his head leaning back on the seat. His eyes were closed, and I realized he was asleep.

"Hey, George, look at this," I said quietly. "He's sound asleep, like a baby."

"That means he's guilty," the wise veteran cop said. "An innocent guy would be complaining, demanding his rights, making a fuss, knowing he is not guilty and trying to convince us. Guilty guys, they do it every time, sleep on the way to the lockup."

While the judge dozed, I called the DA on my cell and told him we had made the arrest and were on the way back. He then put a call to Jonathan Lippman, the administrative judge for New York City, who was not thrilled with the news. Lippman said he would have to get an out-of-county judge to handle the case to avoid a conflict of interest.

In a Rackets Division conference room, Ponzi read Barron his rights while George and I waited outside. When Ponzi came out, he said matter-of-factly, "He wants a lawyer." That dashed my hopes of turning him quickly. It could still happen, but I felt like I'd lost some momentum. He asked for a telephone and called Barry Kamins, perhaps the leading defense attorney in Brooklyn. With the request for a lawyer, we were prohibited from asking him any questions. So for the time being I could not probe him or look for an opening to discuss his cooperating with us.

Ponzi, George, and I were sitting around a conference table with a supreme court judge who had been caught with his hand in the cookie jar. You might expect him to break down, plead for mercy, try to work a deal. After all, who would know more about working a deal than a Brooklyn Supreme Court judge?

But despite doing something stupid and greedy, Barron did know the ropes, and so he clammed up. We booked him, photographed and fingerprinted him, and a few hours later took him a few blocks away for arraignment at the decrepit criminal court building on Schermerhorn Street.

By this time Hynes had briefed his press spokesman, who alerted the media that they would probably want to be in the arraignment court at a certain time. Kamins was with Barron when they stood in front of the arraignment judge, who released the bribe receiver on his own recognizance.

Within minutes he was suspended from the bench but would continue to receive his $137,000 salary while the case against him played out. The media went to town on him, showing pictures of him in court looking dapper in a blue, double-breasted suit, his prominent, wavy hair in place. I had no doubt that sympathetic court officers made it possible for him to ditch the exercise suit he had been wearing earlier that day. Later, reporters complained that he got special treatment from court officers, who stood between him and the media to stop them from asking questions as he and Kamins left the courthouse without comment.

The DA declined comment, but sources reportedly said the judge's entire caseload would be examined to see if any irregularities needed investigation. I hoped that the publicity would bring others who were victimized by Barron forward to complain. That never happened. If Barron had made other illicit deals, all parties seemed happy enough to keep it to themselves. We'll never know.

We started grand jury work the very next morning, and by Friday, January 25, 2002, we held a press conference to announce the indictment of Barron on bribery charges. Hynes gave the public a detailed account of how the bribe demand went down. That afternoon Judge Lippman appointed Westchester County judge Nicholas Colabella to preside over the case.

Over the weekend Hynes called me to report that Kamins had returned the $18,000 on behalf of his client. This was a shrewd good-will gesture on the part of Kamins, who in the face of the evidence would clearly be looking for a plea deal.

Later that day I was at home watching football on the tube when Hynes called again. He told me that he would try the Barron case personally. I wondered who had put that idea in his head. Hynes was a trial ADA when he served under District Attorney Eugene Gold and was a defense attorney, but he had not appeared before a judge and jury in many years. *Not a good idea and more work for me,* I thought.

The next couple of days I spent bringing Hynes up to speed, playing the tape and recounting my meetings with Berenholtz, in preparation for the arraignment on the indictment.

When we appeared in court for that, Hynes was the lead attorney with me as the second seat. Then after Colabella called the court to order, right there, I thought it was a long shot that there would be a trial at all.

The impressive Westchester judge let it be known right from the get-go where he stood on right and wrong when, before any remarks for the record, he asked everyone in the court to join him in a moment of silence to honor the brave heroes of the 9/11 terrorist attack on the World Trade Center. It was one of the oddest moments I ever experienced in court, and I am sure it sent a message to the Barron team. I looked across the room at Kamins, and from the expression on his face I could tell he knew he was finished. They could expect no mercy from Colabella.

Barron pleaded not guilty, and Colabella continued his release without bail. The judge faced five to fifteen years in jail.

Now that the Barron case was big news and Hynes had announced that we would pursue every lead we got that would uncover judicial corruption, I expected a flood of tips about corrupt judges. One Sunday I was having dinner with family at my son's house when I got a call on my cell phone. I did not recognize the number, but I always answer my cell phone.

"Mike," the caller jumped right in, "I'm a court officer. You know me but I am not going to say my name. This isn't even my cell phone. You understand what I am getting at?"

I said I did understand. I got many calls like that during my career. I moved away from the dining-room table into the living room.

"Mike," the caller went on, "you're on the right track with this punk Barron. He's typical. You wouldn't believe what goes on in civil and matrimonial courts."

I told him I did not need his name right now but was totally willing to hear what he had to say. "Who's taking a bribe? Who's giving?" I asked. He had to give me something to go on, a lead to follow.

"Mike, I'm scared about it, you understand. I want to help. I hate seeing what goes on. You got to look at these guys. I will get back to you." With that the call ended. He never called again, but a few weeks later I was walking past the Supreme Court Building when I was approached by a uniformed court officer. I didn't know his name but I recognized him from seeing him in the courts. I thought immediately he was the guy who'd called me.

I stopped walking when he came up to me. He leaned close to my ear. "Mike, I gotta tell you what happened the other day." He told me that the judge he was assigned to in supreme court hearing criminal cases was transferred to civil court. "Mike, he calls his team into the courtroom—clerks, officers, secretaries, all of us—and tells us about the transfer. He says, 'Now we're gonna make some money.' Mike, do you believe it? Stay on these guys, you're doing a great job." He then walked away. Sadly, I did believe it. I say sadly because I loved the law and loved the people who devoted their lives to serving it.

Then, a few months later, Barron did the right thing and

pleaded guilty. At the sentencing a few weeks after that in October, Colabella ripped into him. Colabella said he had listened many times to the secret recording provided by the prosecutor and he did not buy Barron's lame defense that he was a victim of dementia caused by the rare Pick's disease, which is similar to Alzheimer's. He called the judge greedy and reckless. "It was a willful act on your part, a horrendous act, an act that makes me as a judge squirm." Colabella said Barron had made all Brooklyn judges look like "clowns."

But for all the tough talk, Colabella went easy on Barron, sentencing him to three to nine years when he could have gotten five to fifteen. He went upstate, where he spent almost three years. All the time he was in prison, he received his $97,000-a-year pension. When he was released on parole, he took a job in a dress shop in Brooklyn.

We never brought bribery charges against Berenholtz, reasoning that we would have had no case against Barron if Berenholtz had not come forward. Whether he did it out of a sense of duty or fear of being caught, we will never know, but in November 2005, around the time Barron was learning the dress business, Berenholtz was arrested for stealing $63,000 from a former partner's escrow account. Looking back, I wonder if Barron was just too greedy. If he had asked for less, maybe we would never have gotten this case.

In 2007, Berenholtz, then fifty-five years old, admitted to stealing from clients and the widow of his law partner. The disgraced lawyer was sentenced to one to three years in prison by Judge Renee White. She said what he did was "an abomination,"

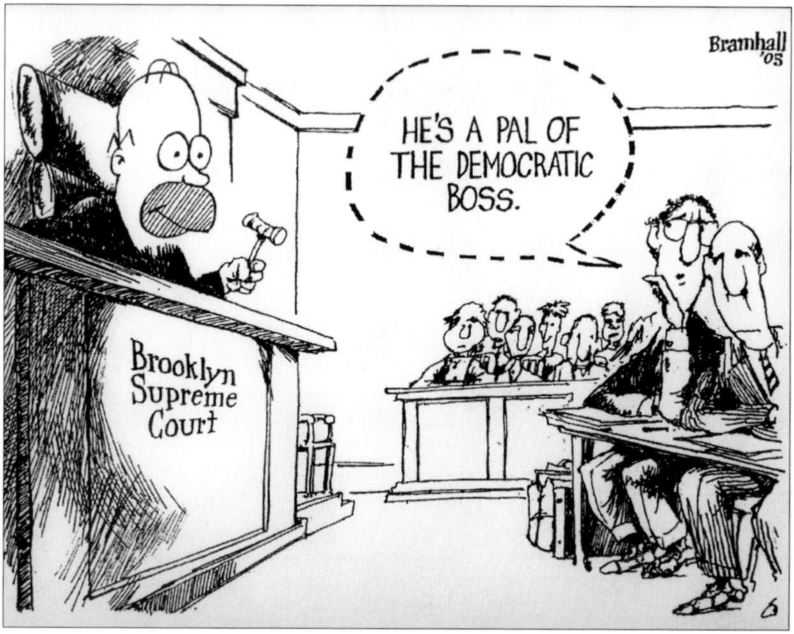

This cartoon by the great Bill Bramhall appeared in the New York *Daily News* in the midst of our judicial corruption trials. It says it all. (© *Daily News,* L.P., New York. Used with permission)

My uncle, Detective Jimmy Murphy, who encouraged me to become an assistant district attorney in Brooklyn, with his wife, Marie, and son, Dennis. (Author's personal collection)

My Mom and Dad's wedding day. Dad was on his way to the Battle of the Bulge. (Author's personal collection)

My sons Brian (l) and Andrew (r) with me the night in 2007 I received the coveted Thomas E. Dewey Medal for Brooklyn Prosecutor of the Year. (Author's personal collection)

My dad, Armando, who everyone called 'Chic" was proud of his service but rarely talked about it. (Author's personal collection)

My sister, Pam, received the President's Medal for her service to the students of St. John's University. (Author's personal collection)

Uncle Louis Longobardi, a Fordham Law School graduate and role model for me, who encouraged me to go to law school. I went Hofstra Law School. (Author's personal collection)

Uncle Freddie Cesarano, a drummer in the U.S. Army Band, who taught me how to play the drums. He and my father had a band that played weddings and Bar Mitzvahs all over the metropolitan area through the fifties and sixties, and played at my wedding in 1971. (Author's personal collection)

District Attorney Charles J. Hynes announces the formation of the Brooklyn Sex Trafficking Unit which was a part of the Rackets Division, the first of its kind in New York City. (Morty Matz)

Sarah Jessica Parker (c) joins me and the sex-trafficking prosecutors. SJP was generous with her time in support of fighiting sex trafficking and recorded a public-service announcement for us. (Morty Matz)

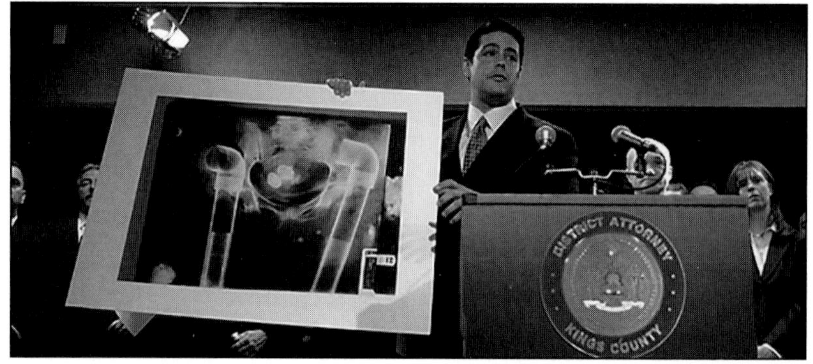

Josh Hanshaft (holding board), Police Commissioner Raymond Kelly, and Patricia McNeil (r). Josh and Trish were the two bulldogs who ran down body snatcher Michael Mastromarino and his gang. (Morty Matz)

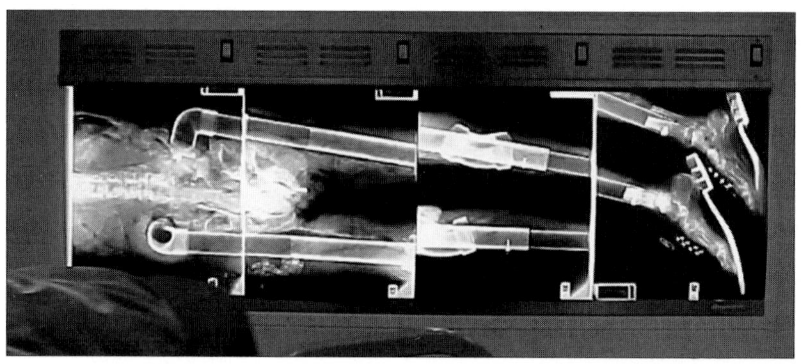

X-rays taken at the medical examiner's office of an exhumed body that had been ravaged by the Mastromarino body snatchers. Notice the PVC pipe used to replace the bones the gang stole to sell to bone and tissue processors across the United States. (Author's personal collection)

BODY SNATCHERS

EXCLUSIVE: How ghouls have been stealing parts from corpses in city funeral homes

MICHAEL MASTROMARINO

A GHOULISH RING trafficking in bones, tissue and other body parts illicitly harvested from corpses at funeral homes throughout the city is under investigation by the Brooklyn district attorney's office, the Daily News has learned.

SPECIAL REPORT

The New York *Daily News* broke the story of the Mastromarino Body Snatching Gang, on October 7, 2005, in the midst of our investigation. The story created a tabloid frenzy. Camera crews and reporters from twenty-eight news organizations showed up for the press conference announcing the indictments of Michael Mastromario and his gang. Two stations broadcast the conference live. The story was a worldwide sensation and documentaries are still being produced about it. Mastromarino eventually received fifty-four years in prison, but in an ultimate example of justice being served, he died in prison in 2013. The cause of his death was bone cancer. (New York *Daily News* Archive/Contributor)

(Left to right) My dear friend, Attorney Arthur Aidala; my friend and former deputy in the Rackets Division, Joesph Petrosino, the best right-hand man anyone can hope for; and U.S. Supreme Court Justice Samuel A. Alito, Jr., at the Rapallo Award Luncheon of the Columbian Lawyers Association in 2007. (Morty Matz)

Judge Gerald Garson wonders what's about to come next at a 2004 court appearance on the judicial corruption charges against him in Brooklyn Supreme Court. He shouldn't have wondered too much, as the evidence that eventually convicted him was all on videotape recorded by a secret camera in his chambers. After a long, drawn-out legal wrestling match and lengthy trial, he was convicted and sentenced to three and one-third to ten years in jail. He eventually was stripped of his robes, disbarred, and served a little under three years. (New York *Daily News* Archive/Contributor)

Former New York State Assemblyman and former head of the Brooklyn Democratic Party Clarence Norman, Jr., arrives at Brooklyn Supreme Court June 5, 2007, for his sentencing on his conviction for grand larceny in a scheme to shake down judicial candidates. This was his third conviction after four trials on various extortion and corruption charges. He was acquitted one time. The once mighty power broker was sent to prison for two to six years. (Associated Press)

Chapter 6

Nothing Beats a Good Cigar!

I was married by a judge. I should have asked for a jury.

—Groucho Marx

The case against Victor Barron and his prison sentence struck Court Street like an earthquake. There wasn't much of the usual celebrating by the DA's staff when a big case is won. Winning prosecutors can expect congratulatory calls from colleagues and friends in the legal family. But sometimes it's hard for a prosecutor who just brought a criminal to justice in a high-profile case to buy a drink in many law enforcement hangouts along Montague Street in Brooklyn Heights. I got some handshakes, but many cold shoulders as well. For a while I was a pariah.

The district attorney called my team to his office to congratulate us, but he clearly had mixed emotions. Barron was not a major player in Brooklyn's criminal justice system, but he was a judge. And while Hynes believed there were corrupt judges, sometimes you can wish you are wrong.

As a kid growing up in Prospect Heights, I had mostly a movie and television image of judges from shows like *Perry Mason,* a favorite in my house. I thought they were like beings from another world who somehow got to sit in judgment of us mere mortals. I accepted their power and authority. On television they were always right and everyone looked to them for answers and a fair shake.

"Tell it to the judge" meant to me that a judge would work things out. A retired judge lived in my neighborhood. Everyone talked about him with reverence. "Hey, the judge says Rockefeller is a good governor and that's good enough for me" or "The judge says the traffic-court guy is on the up-and-up" were the kinds of things people said about him when he left the candy store with the evening's papers. Of course, the judge bought the *Times* while we bought the *News* and the *Mirror.* He was often called upon to settle community disputes, mostly regarding kids who stepped a little out of line with the police. The judge took care of it. And he did not have to worry about alternate-side-of-the-street parking. "No cop would give the judge a ticket," my dad would say.

My first contact with a judge came on my first night at work at the District Attorney's Office after I graduated law school and passed the bar exam. My shift was 6:00 p.m. to midnight, covering arraignments in night court. I dealt with the myriad assortment of criminals, some minor, some serious, appearing in court for the first time on their current charges.

Trying hard to make a good impression on my first day, I reported about an hour early to my supervisor, Bob Kaye. Bob was a good guy and helpful to rookies like me. After I sat around for about thirty minutes, Bob told me that I would be handling arraignments when court resumed after the 6:00 p.m. dinner break. I told him I had never even seen an arraignment in my life. The subject wasn't covered at Hofstra University, my law school. Bob told me not to worry: "Go down there now and watch how it is done." You'd be surprised how much is *not* taught in law schools.

So for about fifteen minutes I watched the wrap-up of the day session. It was a blur to me. I had no idea what was going on. Everything was done so quickly, so pro forma, that without a program I could not tell who was even doing what.

Over a sausage-hero dinner in the luncheonette across the street, I pondered what lay ahead that evening. As every law student does, I had daydreamed about my days in the courtroom. In law school everything you do centers on judges. The law is taught through the reading and digesting of case law. Judges have written all the decisions on cases you are studying. The law student quickly learns about the power of a judge, the scholarship of a judge. Judges are the kings. Their word is the law. It can be challenged, and sometimes they do make mistakes, but on a practical, everyday basis, they rule over the courtroom with iron fists.

I would imagine myself in argument with some of the great judges, courtroom sparring, challenging the defense motions, their interpretations of the law that would decide a case. That was what being a lawyer was about, I thought.

By 6:00 p.m. I was in the courtroom eagerly awaiting the procession of lawyers, criminals, court clerks, and paralegals that would be my community for the next forty years. I was ready to argue. The judge that evening was Richard Brown, who would go on to become the district attorney in Queens County. He was likable and treated me kindly, but arraignment court is like living inside a cyclone.

Dozens of things are spinning around you and you can't put your hand out to grab one. Defendants are brought in, clerks read the charges, lawyers approach the bench, the judge makes a decision. Next case please.

In Brooklyn there can be a thousand arraignments a week, any crime you can imagine from spitting on the subway to mass murder. It's a madhouse, and while Brown ran it well, very little there would make a new lawyer yearn for a career in arraignments. But it is the new guy's duty, and I did it for a few weeks before moving on to an all-purpose court where judicial details of cases get ironed out.

On my first day there I was anxious to meet the judge and some of the veteran prosecutors who might be appearing on a case.

The judge on duty that day was a real veteran. When he entered the court, the uniformed court officer announced, "Hear ye, hear ye, order in the court," and I am sure my heart missed a few beats. The judge looked the part. He was tall with a full head of white hair, and his presence commanded all to stop in their tracks and be quiet. He looked like Robert Young in *Father Knows Best.* His robes were a little tattered, which only made me more in awe of him. *Finally this is exactly like I envisioned it would be,* I thought.

The judge stood at his chair, high up on the bench. The next thing he did brought me back to reality. This picture of American justice took a deep breath, cleared his throat, then opened a drawer on his desk and spit up a huge amount of green phlegm!

Then, as if that were normal behavior, he took his seat and banged his gavel for the first case. It was disgusting. Everyone noticed it, but no one said anything. I was afraid to ask if he did that all the time. I will never know because I never appeared before him again.

So by the time I got the Barron case thirty years later, I was not really surprised by anyone's behavior. But I am forever disappointed that judges are mere mortals. I still greatly admire so many of them. But those years of serving in the arraignment and all-purpose courts served me well.

One thing leads to another. It is mantra for any investigator. *Open every door, look into every drawer. Listen to the tapes. Follow every lead.* You never know when or where the clue will come that makes your case. I made those words to live by. A sign over the exit to our seventeenth-floor headquarters reads, with apologies to Knute Rockne and Notre Dame, PROSECUTE LIKE A CHAMPION TODAY. In the Rackets Division, our prosecutions begin with our investigations.

That's why Assistant District Attorney Brian Wallace listened carefully to Frieda Hanimov when she showed up for an appointment at our Jay Street headquarters one day. Hanimov is one of those people who have a little bit of a lot of places in their character and personality. Many people like her seem to end up in Brooklyn. That is why it is the best place in the world to live and work. It is home to so many different kinds of people from all walks of life. You never know whom you are going to meet in a restaurant or at the ball game or in the lobby of the District Attorney's Office.

Frieda is an attractive blonde with a Brooklyn accent right out of Russia via Israel. She is endearing and sincere. Right off the bat you trust her. She is a nurse from one of the immigrant classes of the nineties that found a home in Brighton Beach and Sheepshead Bay and other, smaller Brooklyn communities near the beaches of the Atlantic Ocean. She's intelligent and tough, prepared to take on the world and take no shit from nobody.

The case against Barron, which Frieda learned about on the television news, brought her to our office and convinced us to launch an investigation into the practices of a major Brooklyn political player, supreme court judge Gerald Garson, who sat in matrimonial court hearing arguments over divorce settlements, as many as two hundred a year. He got that $137,500-a-year job as reward for his loyal party work. He was treasurer of the Brooklyn Democrats, a PAC for the party, and was placed on the ballot for the open position of justice of the state supreme court by then county Democratic Party leader Clarence Norman in 1997. His legal experience before that was mainly as the counsel to the taxi industry, honest and complicated work, but certainly not anything that would qualify him to make decisions that affected the lives of husbands, wives, and their children. Garson's wife and cousin were also judges thanks to their loyal toil for the Brooklyn Democratic Party.

Like Barron's post, Garson's was kind of a backwater in the court system as compared to the criminal courts and even the civil parts where major lawsuits were argued. But also like Barron's post, the position had direct impact on people appearing before it. Just as in the criminal parts, lives hung in the balance of a judge's decision.

Lawyers who worked in Garson's court knew him as a "lawyer's judge," easy to get along with and competent. As the newspapers and television news were trumpeting the breakthrough prosecution of Barron, Frieda Hanimov was in a custody battle with her ex-husband before Gerald Garson. Frieda's divorce proceeding had been presided over by Garson several years earlier, and now her ex-husband was seeking custody of their three children.

Judges are assigned by a random computer process called the wheel, named for the days when it was actually done by a wheel. The wheel had selected Garson, seventy-one, for Frieda's divorce case. But if that was a clean, random process, Hanimov nonetheless felt that Garson was now clearly favoring her husband in the custody battle. And she was hearing around the courts that he usually ruled that way.

For thirteen years, Frieda had been married to a man she painted as a con artist, who, after losing millions in the diamond trade, left her and their three children penniless except for a bag of brilliant, glimmering stones he said were diamonds in exchange for signing separation papers leading to divorce. The diamonds turned out to be zircons. They were beautiful but not worth much.

Now, two years after the divorce, the ex was after custody of the children, based on a never-proven charge that Frieda had hit their eldest son with a belt. So far, all of Garson's decisions were going against her and in her ex-husband's favor. The first time she appeared in court, she was stung by Garson's ranting at her and telling her she had no chance to get the kids, and that she had better settle or she might end up in jail herself, a reference to the alleged hitting of her son.

Sitting in the run-down, almost embarrassingly bleak matrimonial court one day, Frieda complained about Garson to another woman whom she often saw in court, and whose own case seemed to be going well for her. That woman told her about Nissim Ellman. She said he could help Frieda.

Ellman was an electronics dealer with an office and warehouse in the Orthodox community of Crown Heights. He spoke with a thick accent and wore a baseball cap to cover his head instead of the traditional yarmulke.

One day in the courthouse hallway Frieda approached Ellman and asked him about Garson. Frieda spoke her mind and asked directly, "Just what is your secret with this guy?"

Ellman was a character right out of Damon Runyon. He seemed born to the fixer role he played in the Orthodox Jewish community. English was his third language, and he often conducted business in Hebrew or Yiddish and seemed to know something about every case on the packed matrimonial schedule—especially Garson's cases.

He told Frieda he was certain that her husband had paid off the judge, and the bribes resulted in the favorable rulings. Ellman said he knew this because he and Garson were acquainted, and he hoped it was not too late for her to do anything about it. With little prompting, he revealed he knew a lawyer who was close to Garson who, for the right sum, could pay off the judge and get Frieda what she was seeking: custody of her children. (In fact, Frieda's husband was never charged with wrongdoing.)

Frieda was not overcome with confidence that Ellman could help her, and she looked at paying off a judge as something that happened in Russia, not here in the United States, her adopted country. Now convinced that the "system" was stacked against her, Frieda took her story to the FBI and then the New York State Attorney General's Office, where she lodged complaints against Garson.

Both agencies ignored this brassy woman who was accusing a New York State supreme court judge. They treated her as a disgruntled divorcée who was desperate to hold on to her children and would say anything to stall the inevitable.

But the DA's press office had done its job on the Barron case, and Frieda understood the courage it took for a district attorney to go after a judge.

Charles Hynes will help me, she thought.

Brian Wallace was on call the day Frieda Hanimov telephoned the District Attorney's Action Center with her complaint about Gerald Garson. Brian knew better than to be skeptical. I always pushed my people to go the extra yard. It is never a waste of time to listen to a citizen with a complaint. He made an appointment for her, and the next day Frieda was in our office telling Brian and George Terra all about Garson and Ellman and the fixer lawyer.

While some of the senior lawyers in the Rackets Division were dismissive and even contemptuous when Wallace briefed them, Terra's usually reliable gut was telling him Frieda was telling the truth. In his view, the history of her case added up to corruption. George knew no fear, and with the case about to go the way of the FBI's and the attorney general's handling—that is, out the door—George made an end run and came to me with Frieda's complaint.

He also had a plan.

George wanted to put a recording device on Frieda. He loved wiring up informants. He wanted to send her up against Ellman. This would allow us to test Frieda and to hear what Ellman had in mind with regard to paying off the judge.

We kicked the idea around for a while. Frieda, who had remarried, was five months pregnant. That made us a little more nervous about sending her into the lion's den. Any kind of covert investigation is dangerous. We feared Ellman would make mincemeat of Frieda if he caught her recording him. Frieda was not a trained agent nor a street-smart hoodlum. If something went wrong, Ellman might panic, lash out at her, get violent. It had happened before in other cases when a suspect discovered he was being recorded. George knew it and I knew it. No amount of backup in the world could guarantee she would not get hurt.

But Frieda had guts. Her determination to win custody of her children had driven her to take chances before. Now she was willing and eager to take on the New York State supreme court judge who she thought was screwing around with her life.

"I would do anything, even fight a tiger, to get my kids back," she said to me one day. I had no doubt that was the truth.

We explained the risks to her, and the rewards. I explained that if we could get Ellman on tape incriminating Judge Garson, then we could move forward, closer to the judge himself.

Frieda had grown up in poverty, worked to become a nurse, suffered the deceit of her ex-husband, and was not giving up now. She saw this gambit as the last chance to retain custody of her three children.

I overruled those who didn't believe Frieda and gave George the okay to begin. In fact, I took over the investigation myself. Brian Wallace would stay involved, but this was going to be a headline-making case, as high profile as a case could be.

A supreme court judge is royalty in our legal system. I had little doubt, albeit without any evidence, that Frieda was bringing us the truth. I remembered that anonymous phone call that had interrupted me at my son's dinner. The caller had also referred to matrimonial court.

We were starting out on a path that would ultimately destroy Gerald Garson's reputation but also tarnish the entire system. Judge Colabella's whiplashing of Victor Barron would sound like a nursery rhyme when other jurists and the newspapers got finished with Garson. Colabella said Barron made clowns of all the Brooklyn judges. Now Garson would be casting them as criminal masterminds. The stakes were high.

I had no doubt my duty was to take personal responsibility for every facet of this investigation and prosecution, including standing up in front of the jury when it brought in its verdict. Wallace was inexperienced and had never directed a major case. He understood my position and did not take it personally.

Yes, I was aware it would be a feather in my cap if I was successful. At first I would be accused of grandstanding, but I would get the glory if we won, if we uncovered Garson as a corrupt judge preying upon innocent people. Those who knew me, colleagues, journalists, even my family, knew I loved the spotlight.

But if the case went south, if Frieda was bringing us a lemon based on her own disappointments and desire to strike back, as some of my staff feared, if she successfully manipulated me into taking up a false cause, then I would take the heat. I would bear the brunt of the media criticism and the disappointment of my boss for bringing a public embarrassment upon his office. My career would be seriously damaged. But I saw this as my duty. I was the chief of the Rackets Division; I accepted that the risks went with the rewards.

I empathized with Frieda. A few years earlier I had gone through a divorce that left me in a deep financial hole. I moved back in with my mother and father, who were both suffering through a series of health problems. Within months my mother died of bladder cancer, and over the next few years my father had quadruple bypass surgery, had both his knees replaced, was diagnosed with prostate cancer, had a hip replacement, and then suffered a series of strokes that left him with a faulty memory. All this had compromised his ability to communicate, and he had difficulty walking.

The saddest part was that he was unable to do what he loved and had done better than anyone else over fifty years—work at his own fine jewelry enameling business, a lost art, and play the saxophone. My dad was a self-styled Renaissance man. He was a musician, having had his own band since World War II ended. He was a handyman, painter, wallpaper hanger, plumber, and carpenter and could repair anything that was put before him. All this ended with this series of strokes, and I felt it was my responsibility to take care of him. It was more than a handful, but this was the loving, devoted man whose hard work had allowed me to attend college and follow my dream to law school without paying a penny out of my own pocket.

Making sure he got to doctor appointments, seeing to the upkeep of the house, making sure he had food in the refrigerator and that he was taking his medicine, for the most part fell on my shoulders with the help of my younger sister. But that was yet another worry of mine. My sister, Pamela, was not well. She was thought to have multiple sclerosis, which later turned out to be a misdiagnosis, and a few years later died of a rare virus that was attacking her immune system. She was only fifty-five.

So it's an understatement to say that when the Garson case came to me, my plate was full. In addition to dealing with my dad's and my sister's illnesses, I was helping my younger son find a new school midway through his college career. The last thing I needed was a major investigation into a sitting supreme court judge. But that's what I do. And I was going to give it everything I had within myself to give.

Step one of George's plan was to ensnare Ellman. I liked to think that I thought like a detective. George was a detective but thought like a lawyer. Sending a civilian, let alone a pregnant civilian, to meet a stranger like Ellman was serious business.

Ellman wanted the meet to be in the warehouse of his electronics business. Frieda would be alone, with her only protection being our detectives outside, a block away. If there was any hint of trouble, the detectives would only be able to respond after hearing of it over the tiny transmitter Frieda would be wearing.

Frieda readily agreed to the meeting. Her courage continued to amaze me and convince me even further she was not making anything up. She was willing to assume the risks involved. But the decision to move ahead into this dangerous territory was mine. The risks were great but the stakes were high. Thinking ahead to what I would need to bring to court, I made the aggressive call. I needed Ellman on tape. George wired Frieda up. A meeting was set up for that night. We were going to find out quickly whether the Kings County district attorney (KCDA) would be investigating a second New York State supreme court judge in a year.

With each planning session the case grew bigger. I clearly needed help with this case, and in addition to Brian Wallace I added an assistant district attorney from the other side of the world to our team. John Dixon had come to us in Brooklyn after leaving a white-shoe law firm where he had been working since he graduated from law school. John is a New Zealander and felt that his work at the firm was neither satisfactory nor fulfilling, so he came to work with us in Rackets to do just this kind of case. His addition to our team gave us as well-rounded a group as anyone in this business could hope for, and every bad guy should fear. But whether we were going to have an investigation past day one depended on Frieda and her meeting with Ellman.

Before sending Frieda to the meet, we took a look at Ellman. We knew that his divorce case had been presided over by Garson years before, and that the case was back before Garson, to have the divorce decree modified, when Frieda met him. We knew that his lawyer was Paul Siminovsky, who had an office less than one block from the DA's office, so we concluded, for the time being, that the fixer Ellman was touting to Frieda was Paul.

On the night Frieda was set to meet Ellman, she was the least nervous of us all. She reminded everyone of Julia Roberts in the movie *Erin Brockovich*. George sent two detectives to the warehouse to keep it under surveillance so we would be able to see who came and went before Frieda got there. We later learned that Siminovsky was there at Ellman's invitation to get his share of the money Ellman expected Frieda was bringing. That confirmed our guess that he was involved. He was hiding in the bathroom. He did his best work there.

The warehouse was a large, squat building on a dark block. When Frieda arrived, following Ellman's instructions, she rang an intercom at the street entrance and announced herself. To get to Ellman's office she had to walk down a dark corridor about one block long. She said later that was the most frightening walk she had ever taken in her life.

She didn't know Ellman and didn't know who his friends or enemies were. She understood her life was at risk. Frieda walked directly to Ellman's office deep inside the building. She did not pretend to like Ellman. With little in the way of niceties, she talked with him about helping her keep custody of her children. Ellman told her he needed $9,000, which he would give to the lawyer, who would in turn pay off Garson. To prove that he knew Garson and was an "insider," he showed Frieda his cell phone, which clearly displayed Garson's name in the call log.

According to plan, Frieda told Ellman she needed some time to get the money from her father, who lived in Israel. Ellman agreed, and a second meeting was set up for a few days later. After about fifteen minutes the stakeout crew relaxed as they saw Frieda leave the warehouse through the main entrance. The crew stayed in place to get videotape of Ellman leaving.

They got a bonus when Siminovsky walked out with Ellman and hit the jackpot when they captured on videotape the two conspirators embracing on the sidewalk outside the warehouse before going their separate ways. When Frieda learned that Siminovsky was the fixer lawyer, she revealed that he was already involved in her case as the court-appointed guardian for her children. He was assigned to make sure their rights were protected in any settlement overseen by Garson. This focused the picture of a corrupt trio of Ellman-Siminovsky-Garson in our minds.

It sounded to me like a flock of vultures were operating in the matrimonial court, picking over the bones of troubled couples who were trying to hold their families together.

The next morning when George played the tape for my team, we knew that Frieda was indeed telling the truth about Ellman, and the fixer lawyer was Siminovsky. Most important, we had enough to move along in pursuit of Judge Garson.

Now we had to build a case that would stand up to scrutiny because locking up a lawyer and a supreme court judge would be the biggest news to hit Brooklyn since Barron, and the evidence would be examined with an electron microscope. We needed to continue to capture what we could on tape and then advance to wiretaps. It's tough for a defendant to challenge a case when the crimes being committed are recorded for the world to see and hear.

Our next step was to have Frieda meet again with Ellman to give him some money to bribe the judge. We would give him a portion of the money so as to string out the number of meetings with him. Frieda was wired at every encounter. Several days after the first meeting, Frieda brought Ellman $3,000. Just as we thought, Ellman was willing to meet Frieda again to get the balance of the money, which she reminded him took time to get because it was coming from her father in Israel. (Actually, it was coming from the same safe in the DA's office that provided the bait to ensnare Barron.)

Ellman was to be paid a small portion of the money with a promise of more. Now he agreed to bring Frieda's problems to the fixer, Paul Siminovsky. Siminovsky would tell Garson that

Frieda was not such a bad mother after all. His negative reports about Frieda were no doubt somewhat responsible for her problems up to now and would influence Garson to eventually take her kids away.

But Siminovsky was loyal only to who was paying him. The actual fate of the children meant little. Once the money went from Ellman to Siminovsky, the lawyer's stance against Frieda abruptly softened. The loss of her children to her ex-husband was on hold.

We learned all this after Frieda's meeting with Ellman and her introduction to Siminovsky. This information allowed us to develop probable cause to tap the cell and business phones of Ellman. Listening to his calls gave us legal standing to now tap the phones of Siminovsky as well.

Once we began to listen to Siminovsky, it became apparent to us that Garson was clearly in the pocket of the lawyer. Ellman solicited business for Siminovsky by boasting to friends and members of his community that he controlled a lawyer who in turn controlled Garson. Ellman was well-known in those communities, not only as an electronics dealer but as a man who could get things done.

The wiretaps also taught us that part of Siminovsky's routine, once he got a new client from Ellman, was to insure that the case got before Garson. Because the assignment of cases to the judges in the matrimonial section of supreme court was random, by a computer, Siminovsky needed an accomplice manipulating the system to see to it that Garson got Siminovsky's cases. Was he bribing a clerk in the assignment office to insure the placement of his cases before Garson?

"How many legs does this conspiracy have?" I asked George over and over.

His answer was usually a shrug and a twirl around his mouth of his ever-present toothpick. "Who knows? Nobody has ever looked before, Mike."

This override of the judge-selection system left a trail, but neither Garson nor the clerk thought anyone would be looking at them now or ever, so they were not concerned. Frieda Hanimov was not on their radar.

The more we listened to Siminovsky over the wiretap, the more clear it became that he was doing his business, both legal and illegal, with Garson behind closed doors in Garson's robing room, behind the decrepit courtroom and down the hall that was usually packed with angry couples anxiously waiting for their day in court. Although not his formal chamber, which was in the main Supreme Court Building a few blocks away, the robing room in the satellite building, which housed the matrimonial judges, was where Garson spent most of the day. He would arrive there before the court day started, would conduct conferences there with lawyers and litigants during the court day, would retire there during breaks, and at the end of the day would wind down there before leaving for the evening.

To move this case forward, I thought it was imperative for us to have access to that room while Garson conducted his business. We needed to have the room wired for audio and video.

That way we could watch and listen to Garson and Siminovsky commit their crimes.

I ran this idea past some senior Rackets prosecutors who regularly investigated organized-crime cases, the Mafia, Russian mobs, Chinese human traffickers, big-time stuff. They thought I was crazy. The men who feared no bad guys thought that going that deep into a judge's private life would backfire on us. It got back to me that they shared the opinion that it would bring so much political pressure on the district attorney that he would be forced to bring me down; it would be the end of my career. I thanked them for their advice, thought about it, and dismissed it as timid thinking, the opposite of *prosecuting like a champion*.

Now we entered the minefield. Hynes had to approve all wiretap requests before they went to a judge for final approval. He had no qualms about listening in on Siminovsky and Ellman. Frieda had provided enough lead for that bullet. When I told Hynes I wanted to record what went on in Garson's robing room, he blanched and looked at me like I was crazy. A supreme court judge? You suggest we spy on him in his private office?

"There's no other way to do this?" he asked.

I understood why he was hesitant. As far as anyone could remember, this had never before been done. It had never happened in Brooklyn, anyway—and if something hadn't happened in Brooklyn, it probably hadn't happened anywhere.

Our press office had a sign on the wall reading ANYTHING CAN HAPPEN, IT'S JUST ANOTHER DAY . . . IT'S BROOKLYN. Brooklyn was the borough of Murder Incorporated, the Brooklyn Dodgers, the Colombo crime family, the Parachute Jump,

Nathan's Famous hot dogs, Flatbush, the Brooklyn Navy Yard, race riots, kidnappings, fixed college-basketball games, and Spike Lee. And that's just a sampling. Now I was asking a popular, politically entrenched district attorney for permission to bug the robing room of a politically connected supreme court judge.

But Hynes was the guy who'd asked me before he handed me the reins of the Rackets Division if I thought there was corruption in the courthouse. Deep inside he knew we needed to take the chance. He was not a guy to back down, and he nodded and said, "Go ahead, do what you think is right. Follow whatever leads you can. But don't fuck up."

He signed off on my request for an eavesdropping warrant for Garson's robing room. This was a dangerous move. It meant getting another judge to sign a warrant that would allow us to collect evidence that would almost certainly lead to a fellow judge's going down in disgraceful flames. It would taint the entire court system.

Then Victor Barron resurfaced. After the Barron case was over, the then administrative judge for Kings County, Michael Pesce, was promoted to chief judge of the Appellate Term. While technically that was a promotion, it was really an insult as he would now be involved only in lower-court criminal- and civil-court appeals. He was clearly being punished for Barron's crimes, which were committed on his watch.

Pesce's replacement, Ann Pfau, the person I would need to sign the robing-room order, had been in office only a few days when I had the unenviable task of meeting with her to tell her about Garson. Judge Pfau and I did not know each other. I knew she did not have a lot of experience on major cases. Her career was mainly as an administrator in the Office of Court Administration. I was handing her a stick of dynamite, and she accepted it with great care. I was impressed at how carefully she proceeded. She questioned me about how we had got to that point, how certain we were that it would be fruitful. Bugging a mafioso's kitchen is one thing. A judge's private office is another. She did not want to condone a wild-goose chase. I saw that Judge Pfau was a consummate professional. After hearing me out and reading the application carefully, she signed off on our next move. We now had her legal authority to walk across that minefield. We were bugging Garson's inner sanctum.

We had to wait until the courthouse closed for the day before we could get into the robing room. How could we do this in a way that would not arouse suspicion? We couldn't just walk into the court building and tell the officer on duty that we wanted access to a judge's office. That would defeat the surreptitious nature of the bug. Any small hint of this activity that would go beyond our team, especially in the tight-knit community that is our court system in Brooklyn, would blow the entire investigation.

Judge Pfau understood our dilemma and gave us our way in. She told us to see Tom Kilfoyle, the chief clerk on the civil side of supreme court. She trusted Tom and felt that Tom could be counted on to cooperate with us and keep his mouth shut. This turned out to be a godsend. Tom was everything Judge Pfau said he would be. His knowledge of the civil/matrimonial side of the court was invaluable to us, and he certainly knew the importance of keeping his mouth shut about our investigation. He was revolted by the idea of a judge screwing with the lives of the people coming before him. He was loyal to the system he served and was willing to bring down anyone who corrupted that system.

Tom's idea was to go in during the early-morning hours when the building was closed and empty; being the chief clerk, he had a key. So one cold, dark December night George and his electronics bugging team met Tom, who let them into Garson's robing room. Once inside, they needed to find the best place to hide the equipment while not hindering its audio and video quality.

Garson's courtroom was in the run-down, old Brooklyn Municipal Building, not in the Supreme Court Building a short block away. That made it easy for Garson and Siminovsky to operate because no one of authority had an office there. In terms of oversight, it might as well have been in another city.

The room itself was run-down and furnished with institutional furniture. It was sparsely decorated, which at first presented a problem in hiding our equipment.

But the more George's guys looked, the more they liked the room for our purposes. Its run-down nature gave them an idea for hiding the microphone and especially the video camera. Next to the judge's desk was an old telephone switch box from a bygone era. No one would be checking that box for any reason. It was the ideal spot for the audio microphone. It was close to the judge's desk, and because it had been there so long, it was "invisible" to anyone in the room.

For the camera, the nature of the room once again led the tech guys to the ideal spot. The ceiling was covered in acoustical tile, and just above the judge's desk, one of the tiles had a broken corner. The guys thought that putting the camera in that hole would hide it from detection since no new hole had to be created that might arouse suspicion. They worked through the night and had everything in place well before the sun came up, well before anyone else would be inside the building.

We told Tom we needed a spot in the building to set up equipment that would bounce the signals from the robing room to our video monitors and recorders back in a room we called the plant on the eighteenth floor of our headquarters about five blocks away. Tom provided another room on the floor below Garson's courtroom. It was secure and unobtrusive, so no curious janitor or porter or court officer sneaking a smoke would enter. It did not go unnoticed by my team that the room was on the sixth floor and was in an area that had once been part of the DA's office, which was in that building until 1999, when it was moved to the new Renaissance Plaza.

For a few days before the bugs were installed, we had watched Garson to learn his routine. He reported for work at his chambers in the Supreme Court Building well before 9:00 a.m., then walked the two blocks to his courtroom and would typically arrive in the robing room by nine thirty. We began listening and watching.

I was extremely nervous just before we turned things on, worried that something would go wrong and this groundbreaking portion of our investigation would go up in smoke before it really began. My fears were somewhat justified. When the equipment was turned on, the audio was perfect.

The video feed, however, was lousy. The images from Garson's robing room were grainy, and those in them moved as if in stop-action, one frame at a time. This was unacceptable because an eventual jury would not be able to follow the action.

Our equipment was old and clearly outdated. It would not do the job. We needed to buy modern digital equipment that would give us the best picture and sound possible. Blowing the case because of fuzzy video would have made us the clowns of the law enforcement community.

I explained the problem to Hynes, who was not the most technically savvy guy. But he got it. He trusted our tech team and without hesitation authorized me to purchase whatever was necessary. Within a few days when the new equipment was up and running, it was as if we were right in the robing room listening to and watching Garson commit his crimes live on CNN.

The downside was that the tech team had had to return to the robing room in the dead of night when the building was empty except for some cleaning staff and security personnel. They had got away with it once, but could they pull it off again? Any slipup, even the slightest bit of discovery, could blow everything out of the water. Like the pros I knew they were, they pulled it off a second time. Now with the high-tech equipment, including a new camera the size of a lipstick holder that fit perfectly into the hole already in the ceiling, we were ready, willing, and anxious to roll again.

Over the next few days and weeks, we watched and listened

to Siminovsky and Garson conspire to screw litigants whose cases were before Garson and who had Siminovsky as their adversary's lawyer. Siminovsky was totally at home in the judge's private room. He even helped himself to candy from the dish on the judge's desk. One time he knocked it over and broke it. He quickly replaced it. We listened to them make lunch appointments, dates to meet for drinks, early-dinner appointments, and we sent detectives to watch them. In every case, Siminovsky picked up the judge's tab.

One morning during a briefing I wondered out loud, "Imagine if a jury could see these meetings in the restaurant." That's all my guys had to hear. They were big-game hunters with a king of the jungle in their sights. They devised an ingenious way of secreting a video camera in a duffel bag. Then they followed their prey to the bar at the Marriott Hotel across the street from the Supreme Court Building. They got close enough to capture Garson and Siminovsky in living color committing the crime of exchanging gifts for official favors.

Reviewing these tapes back in the office each day got my adrenaline pumping. I was hoping that when we nabbed Garson, he would reject the idea of a plea deal. I wanted him to go to trial. I could not wait to show this stuff to a jury. But I also realized he'd be nuts to go to trial. This evidence was so compelling I could not imagine him overcoming it in court.

On one occasion Garson needed money and Siminovsky called his office to have his secretary bring the cash to the Marriott bar. Our detectives watched as Siminovsky met his secretary outside the hotel, and when he came back to the bar, our camera captured Siminovsky and Garson go to the men's room, where we later learned the money was exchanged. As I eventually explained to a jury, a lawyer, seen giving an envelope to a judge, before whom he practiced, in a bar so close to the courthouse, would raise eyebrows. Thus the exchange was done away from prying eyes in the secrecy of the hotel men's room. Once again Siminovsky did his best work in the men's room.

Instances such as this one, and the cozy conversations between Garson and Siminovsky, proved to us Siminovsky was bribing Garson in return for favorable treatment for both him and his clients. Siminovsky never had to appear on time before Garson as would other lawyers and was never made to wait; Siminovsky got new cases on Garson's calendar with the help of the judge and, most shockingly, received advice from Garson on how to conduct a trial that was being presided over by Garson! That was totally against the rules of ethical behavior by a lawyer and a judge.

Most telling of all was Garson's treatment of Frieda after she paid Ellman. Before Ellman's intercession, Siminovsky treated Frieda with contempt and had nothing nice to say about her to Garson. In turn, Garson treated her poorly and was on the verge of taking her kids away from her. After Frieda paid Ellman, Siminovsky's attitude toward her softened considerably and in turn so did the judge's. Now, the possible removal of her children from her was placed on the back burner.

During the investigation, Frieda, at my direction, went to Siminovsky with cash to offer the judge. We were probing to see what the reaction would be. "In Russia this would help. Can you get it to Garson?" she asked, laying on the Russian accent a bit. Jackpot!

Siminovsky refused to take the bills from her but immediately went to Garson's robing room to tell him of the bribe offer. Instead of reacting with outrage, Garson cavalierly told the lawyer that he should have taken the money and called it a "fee." We now knew that in addition to taking drinks, lunches, dinners, and gifts from Siminovsky, all bad enough, it was even more damning. Garson would take money. We had it on tape.

The more we watched and listened to those two, the more we learned about the depth of the corruption. They were rotten to the core. Their actions in another case bolstered our thinking.

Siminovsky was in the middle of a matrimonial trial presided over by Garson. Siminovsky represented the husband, who was a particularly difficult client. In the trial, Siminovsky had to call a witness to place a value on the business owned and fought over by the litigants. The witness was blowing Siminovsky off and refusing to come in because his appraisal, favoring the husband, would be a guess, and if pressed, he'd find it difficult to back it up. The crooked lawyer discussed this with Garson, who told him not to worry. He would have his law secretary talk to the witness. Siminovsky in turn called the witness to let him know that "the fix was in" and Garson would not press him on the appraisal and, more important, would limit what he'd allow the wife's lawyer to question. All of this was captured on videotape in the robing room as well as on audiotape from Siminovsky's tapped phones.

During this discussion with Garson about the witness's reluctance, Siminovsky was concerned and exasperated because his client was such a pain in the ass, and this witness was necessary to the success of the trial. Acting like his partner-in-crime's guardian and mentor, Garson told the lawyer to calm down. Annoyed, Garson said, "What are you worried about? You're going to win." He said this before the evidence for the husband was completed, and well before the wife's case was even started. This told us that Garson was bought and paid for by Siminovsky. No one had a chance before Garson if their adversary's lawyer was Paul Siminovsky.

In spite of all the great evidence we had collected in the weeks since the wiretaps and camera had gone up, we knew we needed more to cement the case against a sitting supreme court judge. The team kicked around some ideas, such as turning Ellman, but we felt that he would only give us more on Siminovsky, since we never saw or heard Ellman talk to Garson.

We targeted Siminovsky. He had the most to lose if he was indicted or if his sordid scheme with Garson was exposed. Siminovsky was having an affair with his secretary, and we reasoned, if that was exposed to his wife and kids, it would cause him great pain. That turned out to be true. So he was the one to turn into an informant for us. We would convince him to wear a wire as he continued his relationship with Garson.

The plan to pick him up was simple. We had our detectives watching him every morning as he left for work; we knew the route he took from his apartment in Queens to his office in Brooklyn, which was one block from our office. We also watched him during the day while he was in his office because we had a perfect view into his window from the second-floor dining area in the Burger King across the street.

We all had a good laugh back in my office when Supervising Investigator Greg DeBoer called me up from the restaurant to tell us of how easy the surveillance of Siminovsky's office turned out to be. We were getting giddy with the feeling that success was in our grasp.

On the morning of the pickup we followed Siminovsky to work. At a predetermined location, one of our detectives called him on his cell phone pretending to be the phone company. This was to tie up his phone as other detectives pulled his car over. If Siminovsky used his phone to alert his office or his wife or anyone else, our plan to have him work undercover for us would be trashed. He had to live his life as if nothing unusual had happened if he was to carry on with Garson.

The apprehension plan worked to perfection. While Siminovsky was on the phone with Detective Investigator Jeannette Sbordone, other cars ordered him to stop. He was taken from his car and put into a car with George. George told him just enough for Siminovsky to ponder his future as he was driven to the Fort Hamilton Army base, where we had access to a secret office for just such occasions. We needed his arrest to be quiet and secret so we would have the best chance to succeed.

The Army base is in Bay Ridge, Brooklyn, far enough in distance and ambience from the courthouse area that we were confident it would not be compromised. We were set up in an office of the Army's Criminal Investigation Division (CID) because

George had a contact in CID. This remote area of the base was right off the water of New York Bay, with the building surrounded by barbed wire. The day we arrested Siminovsky was freezing with snow on the ground. Because of the remoteness and the conditions we nicknamed the hideout the Gulag. It was bleak and frightening, especially to someone in custody who was not sure when he would see his wife and family again.

Siminovsky was escorted to a room where Dixon, several detectives, and I were waiting. George read him his Miranda rights. He was clearly shaken by the events of the past thirty minutes. He was sweating in the cold room. His eyes were frantically looking around for a friend. His hands were shaking. After hearing that he had the right to remain silent, he mumbled that he would like to speak to me privately.

Once the others left the room, he told me that he wanted to cooperate but needed some assurances. Thinking he was about to negotiate his deal, I was prepared to tell him that only after we received results would we discuss a final deal. I told him we held all the cards, that he didn't have much of a choice to make.

To convince him, I gave him a hint of what we had on the videotape from the robing room. I told him we knew that he accidently broke the judge's candy dish and later replaced it. Then as icing on the cake, I asked him how his son Scooter was doing on the soccer team. He blanched at that. I knew his son's nickname.

Then he surprised me a little. He told me that he had no problem cooperating with us; in fact, it was a weight off his mind, but he wanted an assurance from me that we would not reveal to his wife his affair with his secretary. If I could give him that assurance, then he was ready to join the team. I gave him my word that I would not tell, but warned him that he would eventually have to testify at a trial, and the defense would surely bring up his affair to dirty him up for the jury. That is exactly what happened. But at least he had a chance to tell his wife first.

Here was a guy who had been bribing a supreme court judge, had been fixing cases along with the judge and other court personnel, was facing felony charges and significant jail time, along with the loss of his law license, and all he was worried about was his wife finding out about his affair! *Another day in Brooklyn.*

I was shocked—pleased, but shocked—because accommodating Siminovsky's request was easy. I had no intention of revealing such a thing. With that out of the way, Siminovsky became a part of our team and the debriefing began immediately. He seemed relieved and anxious to help us. For the first time I found him almost likable. Clearly he was clearing his conscience.

Siminovsky had a lunch date that afternoon with Garson, creating a perfect opportunity to wire him up, prep him for conversation to see how our new recruit would perform. It went according to our expectations. Siminovsky actually had a case on trial before Garson. We knew already from watching that he and Garson regularly discussed their trials, without Siminovsky's adversary being present, an absolute violation of all legal ethical rules, but that didn't stop either of them. During these discussions Siminovsky sought and received Garson's opinion on how the evidence was to be presented and received by the judge, and most important he got advice from Garson on how to proceed with the witnesses and what he should elicit from them.

In the days following that lunch, Siminovsky was a regular visitor to our office. We ran into the same problem we had had when we wired up Berenholtz to trap Judge Barron. You could not get through courthouse security wearing a wire. This time, instead of George's switching jackets, he would wait for Siminovsky in the courthouse, then wire him up in the room where we had the transmitter. He would be outfitted with a recording device and sent to meet with Garson either in his robing room or courtroom if business was to be conducted, or over lunch or drinks where a different kind of business was discussed. Just as he did before he began cooperating with us, Siminovsky picked up every restaurant and bar tab when he and Garson were together. They were usually around $100.

Garson never even offered to pay a bill; he felt entitled. The only times Garson would pretend to pay his share of a tab was when members of the legal community were either in earshot of the two of them in a bar or restaurant or close enough to see who was paying the tab. Even those times, Siminovsky ultimately paid. To me, this showed Garson was contemptuous of Siminovsky, that he held him in no esteem, he saw him only as a vehicle to make money.

In addition to Siminovsky's paying all the tabs, he told us that in the past he had given gifts to Garson in return for or in anticipation of help Garson afforded Siminovsky in his courtroom. He always did this in Garson's robing room behind closed doors and only when no one else was present. When Siminovsky was late for a court appearance, Garson overlooked it; when Siminovsky could not make or did not make a scheduled court appearance, he'd only have to call into the courtroom, and Garson would adjourn the case. When Siminovsky needed Garson to rule a certain way or to chastise an opponent, the gifts would ensure Siminovsky got his way. We were told that there was no discussion of its inappropriateness, no attempt by Garson to refuse, or even any feigned refusal. He was greedy, felt entitled, and took with impunity.

We needed to capture this on video. During the case where Garson told Siminovsky not to worry because he was going to win, our plan called for the lawyer to lean on Garson yet again for advice. This time it was with his closing argument. Siminovsky, in the robing room alone with Garson, asked the judge for help in what he should say in summation. The judge then told him what he, Garson, wanted to hear so he could deliver on his prediction that Siminovsky would be the winner. This was extraordinary help because Garson was the only one who would decide the case; there was no jury. After getting the help he had paid for, Siminovsky expressed his thanks to Garson.

The plan called for Siminovsky to deliver a gift to Garson. Garson was a cigar smoker, so we decided to have Siminovsky give him an expensive box of cigars as a token of appreciation. Our chief investigator, Joe Ponzi, was a cigar smoker, so we left it to him to choose a worthy brand. He chose a $250 box of Romeo y Julieta cigars. They were the perfect choice. On the day the cigars were to be given to Garson, Siminovsky and the judge went to lunch. The lawyer picked up the tab, now using our money since he was working for us, and following the lunch, they retired to the robing room. Once they were alone, Siminovsky first gave Garson one loose Romeo, and Garson was so happy to get it he began to sing an improvised song about what a great cigar it was.

After Garson sat down at his desk, Siminovsky pulled the box of Romeos out of a folder and gave them to the judge, saying, "This is for the help with the summation."

Garson expressed his pleasure and, just as predicted by Siminovsky, without further comment accepted them and immediately put them into his desk drawer. My team and I watched the entire event live on video. When Siminovsky left, we watched as Garson took the box out of his desk to take a closer look at it. He then placed it back in his desk and we had him! Independent of the testimony of the corrupt lawyer, we now had Garson on videotape accepting a gratuity in return for having violated his oath of office as a judge.

But now we were the greedy ones. We wanted more. We wanted to pile on. We knew Siminovsky had never given Garson money in return for client referrals, but when we asked him if he thought the judge would take it, if offered, Siminovsky said he was confident the judge would take the cash.

Some of those clients Garson referred to Siminovsky had cases that were before Garson and some not. In return for the referral Garson expected a cut of Siminovsky's fee, anywhere from a few hundred to a few thousand dollars.

In the past Siminovsky was all too happy to accommodate the judge because he was building a practice and who better to refer clients than a supreme court judge. Clients were impressed that Siminovsky had such juice and readily hired him. The corrupt lawyer gave the corrupt judge a fee, in cash, for every client that hired him after being referred by Garson.

This practice was not only unethical, but for a sitting judge to take such fees was a criminal act. Siminovsky told us that before we arrested him, he had been referred a number of new clients by Garson but had yet to give him the referral fee. Our plan was to put $1,000 cash in an envelope and have Siminovsky give it to Garson, telling him that it was for referring the various new cases, and Siminovsky would name the clients to him. This was a calculated risk because we had been listening and watching Ellman and Siminovsky, and Siminovsky and Garson, commit crime after crime. We had a good case, and if Garson refused this money, it could cause us a problem. It could support a future Garson defense that the judge was being friendly with Siminovsky in going to lunch and for drinks and that accepting a box of cigars was small potatoes, but when it came to money, the supreme court judge would never tarnish his office by accepting it.

Was I handing the defense a gift by pursuing this exchange of cash? Some of my staff warned me against it. They understood I am a risk taker. But since the fateful day that Brian Wallace had brought Frieda into our office, we knew we were heading into dangerous territory. *No risk, no reward,* I thought.

We had come far with Siminovsky, and once he began cooperating, he had played it straight. Until now he had not misled us even once. He thought the judge would take the bills. I decided to take the risk. So, holding our breaths and keeping our fingers crossed, we sent Siminovsky to meet with Garson with the envelope with ten $100 bills.

Our first attempt to pass the money to the judge did not work out. The two conspirators were having dinner in Nino's on First Avenue in Manhattan, not far from Garson's home. George Terra and another detective, Jeannette Sbordone, were sitting at an adjacent table with the hidden camera trained on their targets, just as they had many times in the Marriott Hotel bar. Unfortunately a man Siminovsky did not know joined them at the table.

It spoiled his opportunity to pass the envelope. That would look suspicious to anyone. When Garson went to the restroom, Siminovsky followed. But inside his instincts told him to forget about it for that night; someone could walk in on them. The crooked lawyer was showing a real aptitude for undercover work. George and Jeannette got a great meal on the government tab, but the mission was aborted.

George called me at home to tell me the bad news: "Mike, it didn't go down. He didn't pass the money at the table where we could see it. Some guy showed up, took away the opportunity."

"Oh, fuck. Where does that leave us?"

George, never one to panic, followed up with Siminovsky, and we devised an alternative plan.

The following day we decided to try the move in the robing room under the bird's-eye view of our camera hidden in the ceiling.

This meeting started out as almost all the previous ones

had—a little chitchat before getting around to the criminal activity. Siminovsky sat in the chair to the left of Garson's desk, and after a bit of talk, as the video shows, Siminovsky takes an envelope out of his jacket pocket, tosses it onto Garson's desk, and Garson asks, "What is this?"

Siminovsky, as instructed, tells Garson it's for the new cases he sent to him, and he mentions the clients' names. Garson takes the envelope and puts it into his desk drawer, and after some additional brief chitchat, Siminovsky leaves.

The team and I were ecstatic at the result.

About a minute after Siminovsky leaves, Garson removes the envelope from the drawer and counts the cash, laying the ten $100 bills on his desk. He then takes two bills and puts them in his pocket. He returns the remaining bills to the envelope and puts it back in the drawer.

As I watched this all unfold, all I could think of was how this was going to look to a jury: a sitting supreme court judge accepting an envelope, counting the money, and putting two $100 bills into his pocket just before leaving a courthouse where justice is supposed to rule. The playing of this video at Garson's trial was the decisive moment and sealed his fate.

Just then he calls Siminovsky on the phone and asks him to return to the robing room. Our emotions went from euphoria to absolute panic. Was our worst nightmare coming true? Was Garson going to return the cash? Was he not the total lowlife we believed him to be? Was he only a partial lowlife that could convince a sympathetic jury he was only partially guilty? Or would he turn himself into a sympathetic character fighting with his conscience over his relationship with a dirty lawyer?

But Garson did not let us down. When Siminovsky returns, Garson offers him the $800, saying he can't accept it, that maybe it would be better if Siminovsky wrote a check for Robin Garson's campaign. Siminovsky tells Garson to keep the cash and that he would write a check as well. Garson puts the money in his desk drawer. We got him! Now that we had Garson on video accepting the cigars, accepting the money, and essentially guaranteeing that Siminovsky would win the trial before him, we had enough to arrest and indict Gerald Garson.

No longer could any defense attorney say that Judge Garson did not accept money; no longer could he say that Garson was entrapped. Garson was so corrupt that he didn't want cash, not because it was wrong, but because the money would be best served in check form so his wife's campaign could benefit. I had a quick thought about all the honest, troubled people who had appeared in Garson's courtroom seeking a fair shake and equitable solution to their marital problems. I thought about how many times they were taken by this crook!

In conference with DA Hynes, we felt that Garson was a product of machine politics in Brooklyn. He had been treasurer of the party and had received his judgeship from Democratic county leader Clarence Norman; not because he earned it by his great lawyering skills, but thanks to party politics. So if we took Garson quietly, we hoped we could enlist him to work with us, as his favorite lawyer, Siminovsky, had.

What we wanted were other corrupt judges, politicians, or lawyers and any evidence that the Democratic Party sold judgeships! We decided to employ the same strategy that we used on the hapless Siminovsky. In anticipation of the arrest, we began to watch Garson from early morning to the time he went to work at the courthouse.

The Garsons had a dog that the judge walked outside his apartment house, on the tony Upper East Side of Manhattan, in the morning before leaving for work. On the morning of his arrest he walked the dog, then got into his car, alone, and drove off to work.

George's guys stopped his car and told him I wanted to speak to him because he was under arrest. They brought him directly to the Gulag. It was February, so the conditions were similar to those when we had brought Siminovsky there—cold, forbidding, and isolated. Garson did not sleep in the car. George's theory was not foolproof.

When he was taken into custody, Garson was asked to empty his pockets. He was carrying the two $100 bills taken from the envelope given him by Siminovsky.

At the Gulag, George read the judge his Miranda rights and asked him if he wanted to speak. Unlike Siminovsky, Garson declined and asked for a lawyer. We were prepared to bring any lawyer of his choice to the fort to advise him. I asked him whom he wanted, and his choice was someone familiar to me, Barry Kamins. Kamins had been the lawyer for Judge Barron; we had now come full circle! Kamins was a defense attorney of impeccable credentials who would someday become the chief judge in

Brooklyn. He would be a formidable adversary if we got to trial as I had hoped.

We brought Kamins to the fort and filled him in. On a big-screen TV we brought to the Gulag just for the occasion, we even showed him and Garson snippets of the videos where he took the cigars and money.

After some time alone with Garson, Kamins came into the room where we were waiting and reported that the judge would not only cooperate to save himself, but without prompting Kamins told me that Garson could give us Clarence Norman.

The investigation that had started with Judge Barron's asking for money and being convicted had grown to our catching corrupt lawyers and a corrupt matrimonial judge and was now going to put us on a collision course with the corrupt Democratic county leader and number three man in the New York State Assembly, Clarence Norman Jr. We were on the verge of exposing the dirty political machine that ran Brooklyn politics.

Over the next several days and weeks while we debriefed Garson and set up a plan to investigate Norman, we tied up some loose ends in the Garson investigation. After his arrest, Garson could not be allowed back on the bench to decide cases, so with the cooperation of Judge Pfau he was allowed to take sick time, which would cover his absence. We intended to move quickly to wrap up the investigation and then deal with Garson's ultimate fate.

The main loose end at this point was Garson's court officer,

Louis Salerno. Siminovsky told us that he would enlist Salerno's help to get cases before Garson, but he had never given him anything in return. We planned to invite Salerno into our office and question him about the shenanigans in Garson's courtroom in the hope that he would agree to be a witness in any trial that came out of this investigation.

Before we could do that, Salerno, much to our delight, made a colossal mistake. He approached Siminovsky one day in the courthouse after Garson went out "sick" and said he could guarantee getting Siminovsky's cases on Garson's calendar. We had thought it was only Garson's law clerk, Paul Sarnell, who would make that happen. But it appeared Salerno was an opportunist. Sarnell had recently retired, and the court officer saw an opening to make some illicit money at the expense of families seeking justice in the court.

Salerno knew of Siminovsky's dealings with Ellman, and in exchange for his help he asked for electronic equipment, which he knew Ellman could deliver. Unfortunately, Siminovsky was not wearing a recording device when Salerno first approached him, so all we had was his word. I wondered if he was just trying to implicate more conspirators in order to lessen his own role. But he hadn't failed to deliver to that point so there was no reason not to pursue this new lead. We had him contact Salerno to meet in the courthouse to discuss in more detail the deal Salerno was proposing.

Wired up, Siminovsky had the meeting, and Salerno once again told him that he would ensure that Siminovsky's future cases got on Garson's calendar. The cost would be $2,000 per case, but Salerno wanted the electronic equipment now, as a sign of good faith. Siminovsky agreed to the deal and told Salerno, as we'd instructed, that he did have a new case and that he needed a list of the electronic equipment. Salerno told him he wanted a DVD player and some other equipment. Siminovsky said it would take a few days to get it all together.

Several days later, Siminovsky called Salerno and told him he had the loot. They arranged to meet in front of the courthouse. On the day of delivery Siminovsky pulled up in his car, met Salerno right in front of the courthouse, and handed him two large, black garbage bags filled with electronics.

What Salerno could not imagine was that George and his group were in the car in front of Siminovsky's videotaping the entire exchange. To complete the investigation Siminovsky arranged in the next week to meet Salerno, this time in the courthouse, to give him what Salerno thought was the first of many $2,000 payments in return for Salerno's getting Siminovsky's "new case" on Garson's calendar.

Salerno, now showing increasing confidence in his ability to accomplish his scheme, suggested they go into the men's room to exchange the money. While the two stood at adjoining urinals, Salerno told the lawyer to slip the bribe money into his pocket. Siminovsky did just that, and the entire exchange was captured on his body recorder. No one should ever go into a men's room with Siminovsky!

Back in my office when my team watched the video of Salerno taking the electronic "gifts" from Siminovsky's car and carrying them into the courthouse, then listening to the urinal recordings, we could not control our laughing. It was like watching a movie about a hapless thief who puts his own neck in a noose. But in a way, to those of us who loved the law and worked so hard to maintain its integrity, it was sad.

The publicity surrounding this facet of the case was going to tarnish all court officers. Because of blatant greed, Louis Salerno, a public servant of many years, went from becoming a potential witness in our case to one of our defendants headed for prison. I have great respect for the supreme court officers. They keep the place running. They keep us safe. You know they are doing their job when you do not notice their presence in the courtroom. Once in a while a jerk like Salerno comes along and tarnishes them, but in my mind they are overwhelmingly honest, dedicated public servants.

Over the next several weeks Garson attempted to get Clarence Norman on tape when they met at social functions in Brooklyn. He was unsuccessful. It appeared to us that Norman did not like Garson. He avoided face-to-face conversations at social events and would not make lunch dates with Garson. And Garson did not have the natural flair for undercover work that Siminovsky had.

However, Garson was an expert on the workings of the Democratic Party, especially as it related to getting judges on the bench. He continued to provide historical information about Norman's wrongdoings, and this ultimately provided fodder for a wide-ranging investigation of the county chairman. That investigation culminated in Norman's being charged on four separate indictments from extortion of potential judicial candidates to campaign-law violations to larceny. Norman stole from his own campaign.

Along the way Garson inadvertently gave up his own cousin Michael Garson, also a Brooklyn judge—nothing beats political connections if you want to be a judge in Brooklyn—who, while acting as legal guardian for their elderly aunt, forged her name so he could steal her money. We had heard these references on the wire but did not know what they meant. Siminovsky explained them to us. He said Gerald Garson was angry at his cousin because he was spending their aunt's money on his personal bills, and when she passed away, there would be less for Gerald. Michael eventually pleaded guilty, had to step down from the bench and resign from the bar, and got probation. Around the office we took to calling the Garsons the sixth family of organized crime.

After the initial unsuccessful attempts to tape Norman, Garson decided that he no longer wanted to cooperate. He worried that word would get out. His sick-leave act was running thin; soon he would be expected back on the court calendar. Our press office even got a call to ask if Garson was in some kind of trouble. Someone was leaking. So it came time to wrap things up. We had been lucky up to this point. We could have stopped with Ellman. We could have stopped with Ellman-Siminovsky. We could have stopped with Ellman-Siminovsky-Salerno. Now we had two Garsons and were following leads on Clarence Norman Jr.

Garson was arrested along with Ellman, Salerno, Sarnell (who was accused of steering cases to Garson, but was eventually acquitted when he argued that he only did what Garson told him to do), and three clients of Siminovsky's who paid him money to bribe Judge Garson. To protect him and to continue to hide his cooperation, Siminovsky was also arrested and charged.

My Rackets Division was a beehive of activity. We now had to prepare for Garson's trial, and I put a team together to begin pursuing the leads on Norman. We had just been through two demanding, high-intensity years, buried deep in two cases that would make the front pages if they went right or bring us down if they went wrong. Barron went right. Garson still had to be tried.

District Attorney Hynes staged a press conference to announce the Garson indictments. Some of the tapes were played. Even hardened reporters were shocked by what they saw. We really had the goods on this judge. Once again, though, the Court Street community appeared not to approve. Barron was bad, but after a while no one cared about him. After all, he was not a major player in Brooklyn politics. Garson on the other hand was a power broker. He was tight with Brooklyn's long-time political leader and borough president, Howard Golden, and he was a strong supporter of the current county leader, Clarence Norman Jr.

Reporters grew frustrated trying to get someone to say something bad about Garson—something they could quote, that is. At county Bar Association dinners and award ceremonies I found the establishment giving me the cold shoulder. No one wanted to be friendly toward me. Perhaps they feared I was wearing a wire or had them under surveillance.

But one night at a social event I was able to put it in perspective when one of the county's top judges, a real mensch who was respected by everyone, came up to me and offered me a toast: "Mike, you are doing the right thing. Don't back off." That meant so much to me. This guy was the real McCoy, the kind of judge I'd always admired. If he thought this, damn the political hacks, I had to keep my eye on the prize.

Chapter 7

"Just Another Kind of Bling-Bling"

Politics is applesauce.

—Will Rogers

As Gerald Garson rounded up his legal team, our own strategists told me during a status meeting with the district attorney that we could expect at least two years of legal wrangling before Garson would actually face trial, unless he agreed to a plea deal before that.

I could not imagine him not taking a plea, but as a rule you have to prepare for the worst-case scenario. Not that a trial is a bad thing. It is the bedrock of the criminal justice system in a free society. A fair trial is what we all strive for, and I especially yearned for the challenge of arguing before the bench, sparring with the defense, matching wits with the brightest lawyers and judges and overcoming the nitwits.

But from a practical point of view, a prolonged, complicated trial can be debilitating to a staff even in an agency as large and resourceful as we had in Brooklyn. What it does to a defendant is even more debilitating. The cost of a defense is one thing, but the strain on the families, the pressure on the innocents, such as victims and witnesses, is incalculable.

When a defendant knows he is guilty and his lawyer believes the state can prove it, pleading guilty avoids a lot of suffering. That is not to say an innocent person should ever feel pressured to accept a disposition that does not serve him well. But it does happen sometimes.

As head of Rackets, I realized we could take a little bit of a breather, but not much. Noel Downey and Brian Wallace and Seth Lieberman had to prepare for Ellman, Salerno, Sarnell, and the related cases, which would certainly be heard before Garson got to trial. I would be totally involved with them every step of the way. But I did feel a little lessening of the pressure of pursuing two state supreme court judges over two years.

I looked forward to taking some vacation and catching some of Andrew's ball games. He played baseball and football in high school. Both my sons were athletes. My older boy, Brian, was a college football and rugby player and was off on a fine career as a social studies teacher in a Brooklyn public school.

Then I had a meeting with Kevin Richardson, who headed my public-corruption unit. During one of the debriefings with Garson, when he was cooperating with us, he told us that Assemblyman Clarence Norman Jr., head of the Kings County Democratic Party, was misappropriating party funds for his own benefit.

Richardson had issued some subpoenas to take a closer look at the party's records. When he reported what he had learned, I expanded Richardson's investigation. I assigned financial investigators, and senior assistant district attorneys Anne Seely, Jeff Ferguson, and the always reliable Gavin Miles to pour over what Richardson had initiated.

It did not take them long to find among the financial records serious instances of double-dipping, illegal contributions from lobbyists, and what appeared to be a campaign contribution from Assemblywoman Diane Gordon, a check for $5,000, that turned up in Norman's personal checking account.

During the Garson investigation, we had followed a lead that a Brooklyn congressman and a political operative, a lawyer, had asked a judge for more than $150,000 to get the party to support his bid reelection. The money would be used for campaign literature, petition signatures, and what we campaign consultants call "election-day expenses," that is, money used to get out the vote. It could cover anything from renting a van to get senior citizens to the polls, to buying coffee and crumb cake for the volunteers handing out flyers near the elections sites, all perfectly legitimate expenses. What bothered us was that the amount was excessive and the request came with a threat: *If you can't pay, then the party cannot support you.* That sounded like extortion to us.

One newspaper reported that my office was following that lead and we wanted to speak to the judge involved. The newspaper article wasn't exactly accurate, but Kevin and I did speak to some of the people involved, including the judge. However, we did not have enough to build a case of extortion or bribery, which would be necessary to prove Hynes's theory that judgeships were for sale in Brooklyn.

The publicity, while not 100 percent accurate, did prompt another political operative, Scott Levinson, to come to my office and say that he knew two female candidates for judgeships who felt they were victims of extortion by Clarence Norman Jr. When they could not get up enough money to pay for the "campaign expenses," he refused to endorse them, according to Levinson. Without the endorsement of the county Democratic Party, you could not win election to a judge's seat in Brooklyn, as these two candidates found out. Levinson, who ran the futile campaign of one of them, said they would testify in court that they were extorted.

This was a huge break for us. In a relatively short time, the Rackets Division investigators had shifted from looking at judicial corruption to corruption at the highest level of the party, which may have included the possibility that judgeships were being sold by the party leader. We were looking at serious charges against Norman and the possibility of four trials. There would be no vacation for me in the near future.

One day at the office, the same cop who had brought me the Demicco case asked to meet me for a cup of coffee. He had retired from the NYPD and was now working as a detective-investigator for the district attorney. That was not an unusual route for retired cops to follow.

We met in a Starbucks near the office. He told me about a former FBI agent, Roy Lindley DeVecchio, who, this detective said, had too cozy a relationship with the infamous gangster Gregory "Grim Reaper" Scarpa that might have included helping him get away with murder. This particular cop was usually on the money. He said he had a witness who could help make a case.

Several months earlier, he had told me he had good information that would prove two NYPD detectives, Louie Eppolito and Stephen Caracappa, were carrying out hits for the Mafia. Eppolito was a fairly well-known cop whose father was an organized-crime figure and had written a book, *Mafia Cop,* about the dilemma of being an honest cop whose family was part of the mob. He seemed quite proud of his mobster father and other relatives.

Caracappa was a Vietnam War hero who was accepted to the police force despite a felony conviction for burglarizing a warehouse. Police insiders knew him as a quiet, capable detective who kept his own counsel. He and Eppolito were partners on the force for a short time. They were an odd couple, with unusual backgrounds, but it was still hard to believe they actually worked for the Mafia. But my friend's information was detailed and his sources were solid. He told me he was running into roadblocks trying to pursue his leads through the NYPD when he retired and joined us.

The lead he was most sure of concerned the murder of a young man Jimmy Hydell, who took part in a rubout attempt on Anthony "Gaspipe" Casso, a Lucchese family underboss. Casso was the son of a powerful mobster who liked to beat his victims with a gas pipe, thus the inherited nickname. But he also had his own reputation for cruelty and was given the name Lucifer by the US Attorneys who handled his cases.

The hit was ordered by John Gotti, who would eventually

rise to the top of New York's crime heirarchy. When Casso survived the rubout, he swore to get the hit team.

My friend's lead, backed by some dogged detective work, determined that Eppolito and Caracappa were on Casso's payroll. They learned of Hydell's participation in the hit and kidnapped him and delivered him to Casso, who tortured him to death. Before Hydell died, Casso knew the names of the accomplices.

When the investigation began, Casso was in federal prison serving seventeen life sentences plus 450 years. He was being held in New York awaiting being called to testify in a mob trial. We needed him to make a case connecting the two bum cops to the murder of Hydell. I called his lawyer to ask for Casso's cooperation. When the lawyer got back to me, he said the killer would help us if the Feds would grant him immunity in the case. We were willing to offer immunity on a state murder charge in order to use the Hydell case against Eppolito and Caracappa, but the Feds could still have charged Casso in a murder conspiracy.

The US Attorney's Office for the Eastern District of New York, sometimes called the Brooklyn US Attorney's Office, refused to grant Casso immunity despite that he was already serving seventeen life sentences and had been granted immunity in dozens of other crimes in exchange for testimony against fellow mobsters. They were intractable on the subject. I could not understand it. They said they had no problem with Casso's talking to us, but they would not give him a pass on that murder.

My sources told me they were furious at Casso because he had put out a hit on a federal prosecutor that was never carried out. And in a letter to the US Attorney for the Eastern District of New York, he called the notorious enforcer for John Gotti, Sammy "the Bull" Gravano, a liar when he testified against his onetime boss Gotti. Without Casso, that part of our investigation of the two NYPD detectives was at a dead end. We continued to look for other paths that would lead to the truth. It would not be my last encounter with Lucifer.

Even in an agency with more than five hundred prosecutors as we had in the Kings County District Attorney's Office, this turn of events, with so many solid leads on so many major investigations coming forward, was unusual. No one could remember a workload of such proportions. My adrenaline was pumping every day as I parked my office car in the garage in our building. My brain was multitasking, jammed with bits of information I was being fed by Richardson and Ferguson and the rest.

The DA wanted almost daily updates on all of the above. Forget vacations, forget time with the family; once again, as we were since the day Frieda Hanimov walked into Brian Wallace's office, we were pumping on all cylinders. I was going home exhausted each day, then getting on the phone with the DA at night, but the exhaustion was born of honest hard work that employed all my skills. So it was a good feeling.

I constantly reminded my team of what I had learned in law school from a professor I admired. He preached, "There is no substitute for preparation." I drove that into my team, especially as the Norman years awaited us.

I preach the same to the law students I teach at three universities: "Do your legal research. Talk to every witness who agrees to talk. Read every piece of paper you find, from police reports to short newspaper articles that concern your case. Preparation is paramount." Over and over I tell them, "No shortcuts. Make sure you can always hold your heads up, we don't do trial by ambush. Whatever is in the prosecution's file is turned over to the defense." That was the professional code of conduct I imposed on myself while still a law student. I tried or supervised thousands of cases over forty years and I never violated that code.

That is why it is so painful to me that in 2010 the vacating of the conviction of Jabbar Collins resulted in newspaper articles calling me a "rogue" prosecutor who lied to and threatened witnesses. Adding to the hurt is the memory of my father drilling into me from childhood that I should always do the right thing.

In 1995 I was the lead prosecutor when Collins, twenty, was convicted by a jury of killing Rabbi Abraham Pollack, a landlord who was shot and robbed as he collected rents in a Bushwick building that he owned. Another man with Pollack was wounded.

The NYPD did good work. The Brooklyn detectives developed three witnesses. The first said he saw Collins fleeing the scene with a gun in his hand. The second had heard shots and shouting. As he started calling 911, Collins ran past him. The third witness said he was present when Collins hatched his plan to rob Pollack a few days prior to the slaying. No weapon was recovered, and the wounded man could not identify the assailant.

The police brought us a circumstantial case. No physical evidence tied Collins to the crime, and the man who survived the shooting could not identify him as the killer.

Unlike what you see on television where defense attorneys arrogantly dismiss circumstantial evidence with a wave of their hands, juries do not share that view. Many cases are pursued on circumstantial evidence alone, and many bad people are behind bars because of that.

I was chief of the Homicide Bureau in 1994 when the Collins case broke, and the district attorney assigned me to handle the trial personally. He assigned two assistant district attorneys to work with me. One was Charles Posner, an Orthodox Jew who knew Pollack's community well, and the second was a young assistant named Stacey Francscogna, who had done an outstanding job presenting the case to the grand jury that indicted Collins.

The trial jury agreed with the prosecution's theory and evidence, and Collins was sent to prison with a sentence of thirty-four years to life. His original appeals in state court were rebuffed and the conviction and the sentence were upheld.

Collins proved himself a capable jailhouse lawyer, and after failing in the state courts he won a habeas corpus hearing in federal court alleging government misconduct. A habeas corpus hearing opens the door to just about anything the petitioner can throw at the courts to overturn a verdict and to get a new trial. The judge was the relatively unknown Dora L. Irizarry. The district attorney assigned Kevin Richardson to work with Monique Ferrell, who was counsel to the Rackets Division, to determine whether we should argue in federal court to keep Collins behind bars where a state jury intended him to be for the murder of Abraham Pollack.

Richardson and Ferrell's investigation and arguing of the habeas corpus determined that if Irizarry granted Collins a new trial, we would have a hard time winning another conviction. We had lost all contact with and could not locate one of the witnesses, and the other two had apparently indicated they would now give testimony that favored Collins.

One did testify at the hearing on the habeas petition that I'd threatened to hit him with a coffee table if he did not testify for the prosecution at the original trial. That is absolutely not true. At the time I did not even have a coffee table in my office. It just never happened. But Irizarry apparently credited Collins's story, the allegations of his attorney, and the absurd testimony regarding the coffee-table threat.

Then something totally out of the blue occurred.

In interviewing one of the original NYPD detectives on the case, Richardson heard something we had never before heard. The detective said that one evening he got a call from a prosecutor on the case. The witness who said he was present when Collins planned the robbery now wanted to recant his story. However, when the detective arrived at our office to speak with the witness and the prosecutor, the story had changed again. Now the witness recanted his recantation.

The detective had not said anything about this for more than sixteen years. If he had made a note of it or told me about it, we would have been obligated to alert Collins's defense attorney to that fact and would have done so. Regardless of that, the prosecutor present, the one who'd called in the detective, would also have been obligated to note the recantation and report it, even though the witness changed his mind a few minutes later. We would have done so. No ifs, ands, or buts about it. We would have turned over that information to Collins's defense attorney. I have never withheld exculpatory material or, as it is known, Brady material, in my career. No evidence in this case has ever been presented that I withheld anything.

Richardson, who does not miss anything, asked the detective, "Who was the prosecutor present during that recantation/no-recantation session?" The detective did not remember the name. He said it was a male. He said he never made any notes of the session. Richardson then asked if it was Mike Vecchione. The detective said it was positively *not* Mike Vecchione, whom he knew and had worked with for many years.

Somehow the part of its *not* being me has been left out of the newspaper accounts of the hearing and never addressed by the reporters, no matter how many times they have been reminded of it. I don't have a quarrel with the media in general. In fact, I am a media junkie. I read everything I can get my hands on, including every New York newspaper. I watch all the talking-head political shows. I enjoy being interviewed on television. I am proud of my record and knowledge.

From my vantage point as someone the media seeks for interviews and analysis of criminal justice issues, I understand how they can slant and manipulate a story to make their predetermined points. Usually, especially in news conferences about our big cases, I was on the winning side. In the case of the stories about Jabbar Collins and especially his $150 million wrongful-prosecution lawsuit against the city, I believe the reporters followed the lead of Collins's attorney and did not look much past his allegations.

Something else that the media consistently got wrong, especially the editorials, was the assertion that Collins was *exonerated* by the federal courts. That is not true. His conviction was *vacated,* and District Attorney Hynes chose not to retry the case. The only time the Collins case was ever heard by a jury was when he was convicted of killing Rabbi Pollack. But it is true that Collins was "unconvicted" and again entitled to a presumption of innocence.

In August 2014, Collins settled his case for $10 million. I would have preferred going to trial. I believe we would have prevailed.

But what bothers me more than the undeserved negative treatment from the press is the hostility shown toward me by a few members of my own staff and other colleagues at the office. I am surprised and disappointed how quickly some of these people turned on me. These were people whom I mentored, people for whom I fought the bean counters to get promoted and their salaries increased, people whom I helped in their personal lives to further their education and even search for other jobs. These people outwardly showed me respect but behind my back were running to the media to dish hurtful gossip aimed at embarrassing me. It was despicable behavior. They were "anonymous sources." Not worthy behavior by people who earn their livings upholding the public trust.

In some cases I protected the reputations of these very people. On occasion I helped them avoid public revelations of humiliating personal failures. These few displayed no honor, and they are cowards not to come forward.

After the detective's revelation, and because we could not retry the Collins case without witnesses, the district attorney ordered Richardson to inform Irizarry that we would not oppose the habeas corpus petition—in effect ending the case and freeing Collins from prison.

A few months later another federal judge, Frederic Block, who was assigned to oversee Collins's civil suit, after reading mere allegations and not having heard any evidence, blasted DA Hynes and me for misconduct in handling the murder case against Collins.

I did not take what Block said seriously. He was once blasted by the *Daily News* as JUDGE BLOCKHEAD in a blaring front-page headline after he ridiculed federal prosecutors for seeking the death penalty against a drug kingpin. But that did not stop that newspaper from giving him good play when he attacked me.

Even after I retired in 2013 the tabloids came after me on behalf of a convicted murderer whom I'd defended while in private practice in the early 1990s before I returned to the DA's office. The killer, twenty-two years later, filed a lawsuit claiming that when I went back to work for the district attorney, I gave privileged information about him to the prosecutor who eventually sent him to prison.

Total nonsense. Doing anything like that would have been an egregious breach of ethics. No prosecutor asked me for that kind of help, and I certainly never offered it. I told that to the reporter, yet the headline on the story said I was "accused of double-crossing" an ex-client.

The judge okayed hearings on the charges. How do these people get to be judges?

But Collins was not on my plate as we entered the Norman years. Plenty of other issues kept me occupied, both in and out of the office. My younger sister, Pamela, an assistant dean at the College of Professional Studies at St. John's University, was in the early stages of a disease similar to multiple sclerosis and showing signs of muscle deterioration. She had two beautiful daughters, both adopted from Korea, Annemarie and Rachele, who were just starting out on their professional lives. Their situation weighed heavily on me.

Also, my father's health was deteriorating. He suffered a series of strokes that left him with difficulty walking. As a result he often fell. He stubbornly forced himself to go to work each day, by subway, to lower Manhattan from Eastern Queens, but calls to me to come help him home were becoming commonplace.

Years later, George Terra mentioned my father's situation to Frieda Hanimov, who by that time had started a home-nursing service. After the Garson case was over, Frieda was a great help, guiding me through the medical bureaucracy to get my dad the help he needed when he could no longer care for himself.

My days were filled with worrying about my family, planning for the arrest of Clarence Norman Jr., looking into the allegations against a possibly corrupt FBI agent, and dealing with the probe of two retired cops who were hit men for the mob when they wore NYPD blue. It was enough work for any district attorney's office in the nation, much less for just one unit, the Rackets Division, of one agency.

When the day came to fill in the district attorney about what we had learned about Norman, Hynes was somewhat pleased but understandably wary. The Norman team met with Hynes in a restaurant on Smith Street. It was not unusual for the DA to take a group he was working with on a sensitive case out to lunch. It was much less formal than sitting in his imposing office with his top deputies. The informal meetings revealed more of how we felt about the cases. Hynes was on high alert regarding Norman. The man was a political giant, the progeny of a Brooklyn icon. His father was the beloved head pastor of the First Baptist Church of Crown Heights and wielded as much political influence in Kings County as anyone else.

Norman Jr. was admired as well. Right out of St. John's law school, he went to work as counsel to the New York State Assembly Subcommittee on Probation and Parole. What further proof of his father's clout do you need? It was a big job for a rookie lawyer. He went on to be an assistant district attorney under Eugene Gold, coincidentally at the same time I worked there. But we never worked on a case together and were not personal friends.

He then won a New York State Assembly seat in 1982 representing neighborhoods including Crown Heights, Flatbush, and Prospect Heights, where I had grown up. In this huge, diverse, powerful district, Norman quickly became a power broker and judge maker.

In 1990 he became the first African-American to be elected chairman of the Kings County Democratic Committee. He was the number one politician in Brooklyn and held huge sway nationally. Every Democratic candidate including the president, senators, and congressmen needed the support of Clarence Norman.

If your kid needed a job in Brooklyn, Norman could get him one. If you needed some funds for your local senior center, Norman could help. If you needed a permit to use a softball field in Prospect Park, see Norman. He ran the clubhouse, the most basic of old-time political institutions. He could help you or hurt you. Either way, there was always a price to pay. If you wanted to be a judge, Norman could make it happen. He was personable, good-looking, loved the people of Brooklyn, and had a bigger political future awaiting him. He also, our investigators were convinced, had larceny in his heart.

So for Hynes to take him on was as courageous an act as I had ever seen anyone in law enforcement commit to. While his relationship with Norman was always lukewarm at best, it was now going to be trashed forever. If we did not win these cases,

Hynes was finished. Even if we did win, his relationship with his own party would be severely damaged.

He and the people working for him, for any district attorney for that matter, were always aware that he had to be reelected. District attorneys in New York must run for office every four years. They would be fools not to consider the political ramifications of what they are sometimes forced to do. But Hynes did it. He ordered us to go full speed ahead in further pursuit from what we had uncovered. He assured us we would have the resources we needed to continue no matter where it took us.

The investigation into Norman was mostly a paper chase. We weren't planting hidden cameras in a judge's chambers in the middle of the night. We did not have community leaders wearing wires at cocktail parties. In this case, dedicated financial investigators, who know what all those numbers in a ledger mean and whether they add up properly, worked at desks and computers poring over thousands of e-mails, invoices, credit-card receipts, and contracts. These sleuths receive little acknowledgment of their good work, aside from perhaps standing behind the district attorney when he announces an indictment they helped obtain.

Roy Weinstein was the chief financial investigator. He and Vinnie Verlezza, Neil Gillon, and Howard Fortel were bloodhounds on the hunt. They sniffed out every possible lead along a trail that eventually led to four indictments.

The other work in the investigation was carried out by Kevin Richardson, Anne Seely, Jeff Ferguson, Gavin Miles, and detective investigators, paralegals, and clerks. They interviewed dozens of campaign workers, elected officials, tax experts, experts on government operations, and friends and enemies of Norman's in their efforts to get at the truth.

The cases against Norman were heard by four separate grand juries for the four indictments. We then presented charges for a vote all on the same day. The area of the Supreme Court Building where the grand juries sit in secret was chaotic as a half dozen or more prosecutors shuffled through the hallways, their manila folders stuffed with papers, going into the grand jury rooms to ask for a vote.

Norman was charged with stealing more than $5,000 for travel expenses between his Brooklyn office and his assemblyman's office in Albany. He would allegedly submit gas and other receipts for reimbursement by the state while also being reimbursed by the Democratic Party.

He was also indicted for violating New York's election law and falsifying business records when he did not report contributions to his campaign's treasurer. He allegedly asked a lobbying group for the gasoline retailers industry to make campaign contributions in excess of $12,000 over two election campaigns. The limit in New York was $3,100 for Assembly candidates for each election.

And he was indicted for stealing $5,000 from his reelection campaign in 2001 and putting the money in his personal bank account.

Lastly, in what led to the most sensational trial of the four, Norman was charged with grand larceny and extortion by forcing two judicial candidates to pay consultants and vendors of

Norman's choosing or he would not support their candidacy in the 2002 primary. Jeff Feldman, Norman's executive director in the county organization, was also charged in this indictment. He told us he had no policy role in the party, that he just did what Norman told him to do. We believed him, and eventually we made a deal with him to testify on behalf of the prosecution. This facet of the investigation, more than any other, was proof to us that judgeships were for sale in Brooklyn. I could not wait to get this trial going. I knew it would prove the same to the voters.

Before we announced the indictments, Hynes did something a little out of the ordinary. He asked Norman to come to his office on a Saturday morning to meet with him and me.

Hynes and I were wearing our weekend clothes of open shirts and chinos. Norman walked in dressed to the nines, immaculate suit, white shirt, impressive tie and shoes. He always dressed well. He was an impressive guy, not someone who could be intimidated.

Hynes let him know what we were looking at. He told Norman that what he had been hearing around Court Street and what some reporters had been sniffing around about was true. Hynes explained that things were serious and the careers of some people were at stake.

Norman sat passively, taking it all in. I thought it could not be much of a surprise to him. His close friends and colleagues had appeared before the grand jury. They must have talked to him.

At the end he looked Hynes in the eye and said he appreciated what the DA was getting at and promised to cooperate fully with our investigation. He said he had nothing to hide, but then arrogantly added, "We'll cooperate, don't worry about it."

That ended the meeting.

I believe Hynes was hoping Norman would, without prompting, give up something that would enable us to expand the judgeships-for-sale investigation. The DA did not want to make any kind of offer at that point.

It was arranged that Norman would surrender to me at the DA's office at 8:00 p.m. on October 9, 2003. That was a tense day in the office. Reporters and photographers reacting to rumors in Norman's neighborhood staked out the busy entrance to our building, asking everyone who passed by if Clarence Norman had shown up yet. The circus was in town.

Coincidentally, about midafternoon I got an upsetting call from my sister, Pamela, telling me my house, which I shared with my dad, had been broken into. My aunt and uncle had gone to leave something for Dad and noticed that a side door had been kicked in. When they looked inside, they saw some things had been disturbed. Dad was not home so they were not concerned about him,

When I got to the house, they were waiting on the porch for me. "Mike," cautioned Uncle Louie, one of the people who had encouraged me to go to law school, "we just want to prepare you. It is a mess in there. It's disgusting."

I carefully opened the front door and walked into the living room. The downstairs of the house was my father's domain. I had a separate apartment on the second floor. His area did not seem so bad to me. The television was there, a record collection, an extensive coin collection, some bric-a-brac collected over fifty years of marriage—all was where it belonged. Nothing seemed to be missing.

When I got to the second floor, my apartment, what I walked into took my breath away. The entire suite of rooms had been ransacked. Every single dresser and desk drawer had been opened and the contents thrown on the floor. All my files, personal papers, had been dumped. The clothes from my closet were thrown all over the place. It looked like a tornado had hit it.

The first thing I looked for was an envelope with $2,000 in cash I was saving for Christmas presents. It was gone. Next, with my heart pounding, I searched for a briefcase I had hidden in a closet. It held $4,000 earmarked for Andrew's tuition. I was almost afraid to look when I opened the briefcase, but the money was there. Somehow the burglar missed it. But he did not miss my collection of watches, worth about $5,000. They were gone.

My shield collection was also gone. Most people in law enforcement save the shields, or badges, they were issued as they moved up through the ranks in the DA's office or the police department. You will probably see some kind of display showing those shields that distinguish their careers in their offices or in their homes when they retire. I'd had shields starting from when I was a brand-new assistant district attorney, then a deputy bureau chief, bureau chief, executive assistant district attorney—all were taken by the burglar. The only one that hadn't been taken was the one with four stars, chief of the Rackets Division. I felt for the case to make sure it was in my pocket. I took some comfort that it was.

I went back downstairs, where my uncle Freddie—my late mother's brother, a musician who'd taught me how to play the drums—had arrived. My two uncles, anxious to be of help, were fixing the side door. I continued my survey of the damage by going to the basement.

It was like stepping into a nightmare. Again, everything a person could get his hands on was emptied and overturned. And the floor was soaked because the toilet had been stuffed with paper and then flushed so it would overflow. I realized then that this was a personal attack on me because before the burglar flushed the toilet, he used it. He left his calling card. It was disgusting and I took it personally, as it was clearly meant to be.

But who was sending me a message? Police came and dusted for fingerprints, and they agreed it seemed to be the work of a pro. That burglar was never caught. We never did get to the bottom of it. I had to bring in an industrial cleaning crew to make the basement livable again.

Meanwhile, I had to get back to the Norman surrender. At the office when I confided to my close friends what had happened, those who knew about the Eppolito-Caracappa investigation quickly attributed the break-in to them. It would have fit their MO. But who knows?

Norman came in on time with his lawyer, after eating dinner at the Park Plaza diner, where Brooklyn Democrats often held lunch and dinner functions, with a group of supporters including most of the county's district leaders. Detectives took Norman in for processing. Photos, fingerprints, records check, and other paperwork needed to be completed before court the next morning.

I laid out the charges included in the four indictments. I also allowed Norman to spend the night in our offices on the eighteenth floor rather than being taken to the holding cells at central booking with the hundreds of other criminal suspects awaiting arraignment in the morning.

The next morning we went over to Supreme Court, where a throng of his supporters awaited him to lift his spirits. When he walked into the courtroom, Norman lifted his hands to show the handcuffs and arrogantly said to his friends, "Just another kind of bling-bling." The picture made the front pages and we were off to the races.

About three weeks later, I went for an early-morning workout as was my habit. I returned home about 6:00 a.m. and parked in my driveway as usual. I went inside to shower and shave and get dressed for the office.

When I came out, I saw immediately that the back window of my office car, a new Chevy Impala, was totally smashed in. There was no other damage to the car and nothing appeared to have been stolen. I looked up and down the block to see if my neighbors and I had been the victims of vandalism. No other car appeared to be damaged.

I was shaken. Was this another message? Two days later it became more clear that I was being targeted. My office arranged for the car to be repaired in a local body shop. The shop called George Terra and asked him to come down to see something they had found in the roof of the car above the smashed window.

George called me from the shop. "Mike, do you smoke?" He knew I didn't and I reminded him of that. "No, I mean, smoke, you know, smoke."

I understood where he was going. "You mean dope, marijuana?"

"Yeah, Mike. The repair guys found a big bag of marijuana hidden in the ceiling near the rear window. Is it yours?"

I was too nervous to laugh. "It's not mine, George. You know me better than that."

"I figured so, but whoever broke your window, and I'll bet it's the same guy who stuffed your toilet, is giving you another reminder. I'll start an investigation."

Of course we filled in the district attorney and the police department. Hynes again ordered round-the-clock bodyguards as he did during the Demicco investigation. But this time even surveillance cameras were installed at my house as well as a "panic" button that, when pushed, would alert the local precinct that I needed their help. But we never found the culprit.

Now, I had the Norman trials beginning, Garson appeals being argued in preparation for his trial, early suspicions that an FBI agent had gone wrong, and two crooked NYPD detectives warning me to stay out of their business.

Chapter 8

He Needed Just Twelve More Votes

All truths are easy to understand once they are discovered; the point is to discover them.

—Galileo

Bronx judge Martin Marcus, who had a reputation as a legal scholar, was assigned to handle the Norman trials. He was facing at least one year of presiding over a politically charged courtroom dealing with sensational cases. He was eager to get started and called us in for a conference on which trial would come first.

I was hoping to start with the double-dipping case because to me it was the most straightforward, nothing tricky about it. Norman billed the state for money his party had already reimbursed him. But the case was stalled in appeals, much like the Garson case, for more than a year as Norman's lawyers argued over the charges.

So we decided to move forward on what we called the lobbying case, the charge that Norman had violated New York's election law by soliciting and receiving more than $12,000 in campaign contributions, from a gasoline-industry lobbying group in two elections, when the limit would have been $3,100 for each. He also falsified records by keeping the contributions secret from his own campaign treasurer. The campaign treasurer and officials of the lobbying group testified for the prosecution, offering no help to Norman.

Norman and his lawyer, Edward Rappaport—a former judge who was my supervisor when I was a young assistant in the DA's Investigations Bureau, and was a fixture in Brooklyn's court system—decided to let the assemblyman testify on his own behalf. Rappaport's direct examination made clear that their strategy was twofold: they would blame everyone but Norman, and Norman would win over the jury with his personality.

He could be charming. An experienced campaigner, he had won twelve elections and knew how to get people's votes. Now he needed to convince twelve members of the jury to vote for him. He must have thought it would be a snap.

Norman's testimony took up most of the morning, and I began my cross-examination as soon as he was finished. I understood Norman would be a formidable opponent. This case could rise or fall on his credibility despite the evidence, which consisted mainly of canceled checks and testimony from rather bland witnesses who said Norman asked them for more money than the law allowed and they, believing he knew the law, gave it to him.

Prior to court in the morning, I gathered Richardson and Ferrell in my office, and we went over everything, prepared to counter Norman's testimony. We knew that not only this trial but the three trials to follow would depend on the outcome of what happened this day between Clarence Norman and me. It would set the tone for everything that followed.

Norman was a nationally known and respected political figure, probably the most famous person, other than a notorious killer, I had ever had on the stand. This was the spotlight I'd craved all my life, and I understood the consequences of failure. If he was too slick for me to nail, we were cooked. Hynes's political career would be over and I would be a pariah on Court Street.

My strategy was to ask simple, pointed questions and not give him a chance to elaborate or make speeches to the jury. I wanted him to look me in the eye and say he did not know the law or that someone else made a mistake. I did not want him to engage the jury as he had successfully done under Rappaport's softball questioning.

In my cross-examination I employed a technique I had learned over thirty years of trying cases, which was not the kind of thing you learned in law school. Earlier, when being questioned by his own attorney, Norman had looked at the jury when he answered. He was playing for their sympathy and understanding, like a politician playing to the crowd. But I positioned myself on the right side of the podium, in the center of the courtroom and to Norman's left. As I asked questions from this position, Norman would have to turn his head to look at the jury as he answered. It appeared awkward and phony and weakened his game.

Rappaport had been battering home the notion that the

District Attorney's Office was "criminalizing politics." My task was to make Norman sound like he *was* a criminal, not a politician.

He offered the lame defense that he did not know the law regarding limits on contributions, and that his campaign treasurer, a competent woman and good friend of Norman's, made mistakes in her entries. Norman was charming, charismatic, and almost believable. It's a risky move for a defendant to take the stand to face examination by the prosecutor, but I believe he did well in an attempt to argue stupidity as opposed to larceny. But it was a ridiculous argument. After a tense couple of hours of this, I knew I had won the day.

I was drenched in sweat as I spoke to television reporters in the hallway following that session. They threw questions at me about Rappaport's "criminalizing politics" attack. I answered with what I had established in the courtroom. Norman knew the rules. He helped write the rules. Breaking them was a criminal act.

When I summed up at the end of the trial, I reminded the jury that Clarence Norman Jr. was fifty-four years old at the time of the alleged crime and was a smart, accomplished son of Brooklyn. He graduated Howard University in three years. He had graduated St. John's Law School and passed the bar exam on his first try. He had been an assistant district attorney for five years handling all kinds of serious cases. He was now deputy speaker of the New York State Assembly, and the head of the Brooklyn Democratic Party. He was polished, intelligent, and, as he himself had testified, careful in his business dealings. The icing on the cake: for twenty-three years he'd served on the Assembly

Election Law Committee, which passed the law that he now claimed to know nothing about. He was at the time the senior member of the committee.

I asked the jury how they could believe he did not know the law governing how much he could ask for and receive in campaign contributions. Of course he knew what he was doing!

On September 27, 2005, the jury found Norman guilty. He faced four years in prison but Judge Marcus had decided to postpone any sentencing until all the trials were completed.

In speaking with some jurors following the trial, we found that they just did not like politicians. The more he campaigned to win their votes, the worse it got for him. No matter how charming and pleasant Norman was on the stand, they viewed him as a politician who could not be trusted. I thought this served us well as we headed into the remaining trials.

A few weeks after the lobbying trial, I asked Norman and Rappaport to come up to my office. Kevin Richardson joined us. As always, Norman was impeccably dressed and radiating arrogance. I laid out the facts of the three upcoming trials and what Norman would face if he was convicted. Norman sat, chewing gum, seemingly bored. I raised the possibility of his helping us with our judicial-corruption investigation. Perhaps, I offered, his cooperation would sit well with a judge and he could avoid serious jail time.

He took it all in. He offered no reaction, but I knew he understood; he was, after all, a former assistant district attorney in Brooklyn. In a long, awkward silence, the four of us just looked straight ahead. Finally, the weary veteran Rappaport broke the spell: "We don't know anything." They left, and Kevin and I shrugged and went back to work.

With still no movement on the double-dipping charges Marcus urged us to keep moving ahead, and in December we began the stolen-check trial.

Once again, Rappaport was his lawyer and Norman took the stand in his own defense. His act was the same. He tried to blame everyone but himself. He used all his charms to try to sway the jury.

I was a little more relaxed when I cross-examined him this time. I gave him a little more room to turn it on. I knew the jurors would reject the politician as they had in the first trial. I was not sweating bullets that day when I met the reporters in the hallway.

After deliberating for almost a week, the jury found Clarence Norman Jr. guilty of grand larceny and falsifying records for personally cashing a $5,000 check in October 2001 written by the Thurgood Marshall Political Club as a contribution to his re-election committee. Rappaport argued that the money Norman pocketed was payback of a loan on behalf of the club he made to Assemblywoman Diane Gordon to pay election workers in the 2001 race for comptroller.

Rappaport, fishing for any help he could get, even called Diane Gordon as a defense witness. But in a hearing prior to her testimony, and with the jury not in the courtroom, she said she would plead the Fifth Amendment if called to testify. Perhaps she was afraid she would incriminate herself. Richardson and I were sure that if she had anything to say that would have helped

Norman, such as that he'd actually made such a loan, then she would have tried to bail out her pal. But she could not testify to that because no evidence supported it.

On the stand Norman was blaming everyone he could think of, saying the money was mislabeled a "contribution" when it should have said "reimbursement." He threw everyone under the bus. He even dissed his close associates, people who were his strongest supporters and hardest workers in Thurgood Marshall and the Democratic Party. He testified his close friend Charles Dyer, the party treasurer, was "merely competent." He denigrated them all.

Their own testimony proved them all to be aboveboard, competent, and law-abiding. They were detailed, meticulous, and principled. After all, they were at the controls of the largest Democratic organization in the country, and unlike Norman, they took their fiscal responsibilities seriously. It was sad, I thought, that they had to hear a man they admired and were devoted to put them down as he tried to save his own skin.

The check in question, from Diane Gordon, was a contribution to the election committee, and that is how they labeled it. It was not meant for Norman's personal use, and his friendly banker should not have cashed it for him.

In my closing argument, I likened Norman to a magician who could make you believe he made an elephant disappear from a room by his skill at misdirection. But Norman was no Houdini and this was not an arena of make-believe. The jury saw copies of the check inappropriately, to say the least, deposited in Norman's personal account. They heard testimony that he had it transferred to a bank in Albany before he actually cashed it. Roy Weinstein's financial investigators had found the paper trail.

The day I summed up was about one week after the commemoration of the twenty-fifth anniversary of the murder of John Lennon. I used Lennon's words from his song "Gimme Some Truth" to close my summation:

I've had enough of reading things by neurotic, psychotic,
pigheaded politicians.
All I want is the truth . . .

I could tell by the silence in the courtroom when I finished that the jury got my point.

No one supported Norman's claim.

After about one week of deliberation, longer than I thought it would take, which made me a little nervous, the jury returned guilty verdicts on two felony counts. On this conviction, Norman faced up to fifteen years in prison, and Judge Marcus, now rightfully concerned that Norman had reason to skip the country rather than return for sentencing, responding to our request, raised his bail from the original $25,000 after his first trial to $100,000.

Norman's family could not raise that amount of money quickly, and a bizarre afternoon passed as the judge allowed Norman to sit in the courtroom with his family for hours while they made the arrangement for the additional money.

With Norman's two trial convictions in a year and his facing serious prison time, the Court Street insiders were speculating like crazy, and some were running for cover. The press would not let anyone forget that the Norman investigations grew out of our probe of "judgeships for sale in Brooklyn." Word was that Norman, still facing two felony trials, would now roll over.

I find it odd that so many people simply accepted that judges bought their way onto the bench. Newspaper columnists, especially the great Jack Newfield, railed on about how a system of selecting judges that produced the likes of Victor Barron and Gerald Garson was corrupt enough to sell seats on the bench.

Sure enough, tips flooded into my office, mostly anonymous, but some from respected lawyers and an occasional journalist, which kept my assistant prosecutors, detective investigators, and financial investigators busy around the clock. One informant told us that a judge had bragged about paying $50,000 to buy his seat on the bench. The informant said he was willing to wear a wire and get the judge in conversation. He was certain the judge would confirm it on tape. We set things up, but it never went anywhere; we could not get this bragging judge on tape.

In March 2006 we finally got the double-dipping case to trial. We always believed this was a no-brainer. We charged that Norman ripped off $5,800 from taxpayers when he asked for and received reimbursement for his traveling expenses from his Brooklyn office to his office in Albany. It is a legitimate expense, except that Norman was also being reimbursed for those trips by the Brooklyn Democratic Party.

Norman did not take the stand, so the State Assembly

Speaker, Sheldon Silver, reluctantly became the star witness. He testified that he would not have offered travel vouchers for expenses he did not pay for. But Silver did not have jurisdiction over the reimbursements, and Judge Marcus reminded the jury that the Speaker was not an expert.

Despite the paperwork evidence clearly showing Norman was reimbursed twice for the same expenses, the jury voted to acquit. He beat that rap, I think, mainly because the jury did not fully understand the charges, as simple as they sounded to us. When the judge "charged" the jury—that is, explained the charges to them before they began deliberations—I believe they became confused about whether it mattered that Norman did actually lay out money from his pocket before he was reimbursed by the Assembly. The jury foreman was a banker, and from what we learned from speaking to the jurors after the trial, she guided them to the acquittal. No matter, they acquitted him and that was final. The prosecution does not get to appeal a verdict.

Jury selection is the key to any trial strategy. These Norman trials were undeniably carried on in a racially charged atmosphere. Many Brooklyn residents and some of the press believed that if Norman were a white politician, the alleged crimes would have been overlooked by the district attorney.

That was rubbish as far as I was concerned. But we could not ignore that pretrial publicity may have influenced the jury pool, and that attitudes about race—and in Brooklyn everyone has an attitude about everything—would have to be met head-on.

A few weeks before the first trial Hynes had suggested we hire a jury consulting firm to work with us in plotting how we would select our jurors. Richardson, Ferrell, and I spent a day at the firm's Long Island office listening to the evidence from their experience, polling, and focus groups. Of all the things they had to share with us, the only eye-opener was how little people knew about Norman as an individual and about the case as a whole. Few of their sample groups, all Brooklynites, knew who he was. And few knew anything about the case at all, this after weeks of major tabloid headlines.

They reached the same conclusion we had. Pick a middle-of-the road jury, solid citizens. Look for homeowners, people in stable jobs with long work histories; don't avoid minorities even though in some communities Norman was thought of as a hero. All that really mattered was that Norman was a politician, and people do not trust politicians.

Following the third trial, I spent a few weeks catching up on office paperwork and personnel matters. I was in charge of a large division, and my prosecutors were always busy with one thing or another.

In fact, Noel Downey was hard on the heels of Roy Lindley DeVecchio, the FBI agent we were investigating for allegedly helping mob killer Gregory Scarpa murder four people. That investigation was moving toward indictments. And by this time we had already built a case against the two Mafia cops, Louie Eppolito and Stephen Caracappa, who were hit men for the mob. Because the Drug Enforcement Administration was in the middle of a drug-dealing investigation of the two dirtbags, we agreed to turn over all we had to the Feds, and they prosecuted the two. Both were convicted in federal court and sentenced to life in prison.

No more overt threats had been made against me since the break-in, so the bodyguards were gone. The investigation into the culprit pretty much ended after a precinct detective suggested I visit pawnshops in Jamaica, Queens, to see if I could spot any of the stolen watches. I figured the police were dead in the water if they needed me to do that.

But if things were easing a bit in the office, on the home front pressures were building. My sister Pamela's condition had worsened. She could not focus on her job, and one morning she fell while at work. She finally agreed she had to take a leave of absence.

And my father was sinking as well. He continued to have small strokes. One of his doctors took the time to show me pictures of his brain, which showed an increasing number of black spots. The doctor explained those spots indicated his brain cells were being destroyed by the strokes. This once-vibrant man, a skilled artisan, musician, and family man who loved life, a World War II combat veteran who was awarded the Bronze Star for heroism, now spent his days in a chair or in bed. It was heartbreaking to me and constantly on my mind.

Chapter 9
Crying in Court

County can make you or County can break you.

—JUDGE MARGARITA LOPEZ TORRES

ON JANUARY 23, 2007, for the fourth time in two years, a jury sat waiting for opening statements in a case against Clarence Norman Jr. When I briefed Hynes a few days before, I told him that this trial, no matter the outcome, would be the most explosive of the four and the most supportive of his theory that judgeships could be bought in Brooklyn. I fully expected testimony that would reveal the political underbelly of our community and leave a bad taste in everyone's mouth. I also expected the race question to permeate all discussion of the case, in and out of the courtroom.

Despite the discussion about race outside the courtroom, up to now Norman's lawyers had not overtly brought race into their questioning, their openings, or their closing arguments. In sidebar discussions with the judge it was rarely mentioned; there was no caution from Marcus. It had, up to now, been more or less a clean fight. That would now change.

The feverish atmosphere around this case in the media had not existed in the previous trials. I was feeling it in my own office. No one would confront me head-on, but I knew some people supported the notion of Norman as victim. Despite its being the most important case in the office, rarely did anyone ask me how it was going. It was as if they were afraid there would be political consequences.

Kevin Richardson got things rolling with our opening statement. He came out fighting, aggressive, no holds barred. He called Norman the "undisputed boss of Brooklyn politics." He said Norman knew how to use words as bullets and knives, and his words could be as "hurtful and destructive as bombs." The opening took up the entire morning session.

Right after lunch, from the first words of the defense attorney's opening to the jury, I was proven correct as the defense steered the jury, which included eight minorities, to look at the racial overtones of the case. Anthony L. Ricco, an African-American, a rising young star in the defense bar, compared Norman to Martin Luther King Jr. He called his client a civil rights warrior who was actually standing up to two judicial candidates who aimed to deny black voters their freedom of choice. Mr. Norman, he told the jurors, was not extorting the two female judges prosecutors portrayed as victims. Instead, Ricco said, Norman "tried to inspire them beyond their own ignorance."

Ricco invoked "Letter from Birmingham Jail," written by King in 1963 after he was arrested in a civil rights demonstration that consisted mainly of marches and sit-ins. Sitting at the prosecutor's table, I thought Ricco stuck a brilliant chord. Norman by now had two felony convictions on his plate and was facing serious prison time. It was fair to call him a criminal. But Ricco did not agree. Being jailed did not mean King was a criminal, nor did it mean Norman was.

As Ricco, a professorial-looking man with a bow tie and glasses, went on and on, I started writing my summation in my head even though it was weeks away. During the trial Richardson and I would have to hammer home that Norman was not a warrior, but a thief and a bully. He was not a man who cared as much for his community as he did for his own exercise of power.

In a nutshell, the indictments for this case charged that Norman strong-armed two candidates for civil court judgeships, Karen B. Yellen and Marcia J. Sikowitz, by threatening to withdraw the support of the Kings County Democratic Party, which Norman headed, if they did not hire, as the *New York Times* put it, "his pet consultants and cronies to run their campaigns." The two women were basically told to run together and come up with money, spend it where Norman wanted it spent, or get lost. This was first brought to our attention by campaign consultant Scott Levinson after he read that slightly inaccurate newspaper story about our fledgling investigation into judgeships for sale.

I was not worried about parrying the race card. We had plenty of ammunition on our side. Two of our witnesses against

Norman had histories of activism in the civil rights movement, and Norman himself had shown he would exploit racial perceptions as willingly as anybody else.

"My way or the highway" was Norman's slogan. Each day, with each prosecution witness, Richardson and I were building the idea that Clarence Norman Jr. in no way belonged in the same sentence as Martin Luther King Jr.

In opening statements, a defense lawyer or prosecutor is supposed to tell the jury what he plans to prove either on behalf of his client or against the defendant. Opening statements are supposed to be a road map of the upcoming trial. Ricco's opening appeared to have no facts to support it. When he brought in testimony that in the 2002 judicial race Norman backed a slate of three Jewish women, it sounded like more racial manipulation than fairness or a search for quality.

The jurors and the public were hearing that in politics decisions were based on how much money you could deliver to the party and whom you could help stay in power. During national election years the news is filled with reports of how much money candidates are raising. The candidate who raises the most has a decided advantage. In national elections the number of dollars can go into the hundreds of millions. It is used mostly to fund television ad campaigns, top-level campaign staffing, and thousands and thousands of direct-mail items to voters' homes. In Brooklyn politics the numbers were not nearly as astronomical, but relatively speaking they were just as difficult to raise.

When we put Scott Levinson—the head of the Advance Group, Yellen's political consulting team, and the man who first tipped us to Norman's extortionist methods—on the stand, he provided an inside look at the kind of negotiations that the county boss directed. Levinson testified that in the week leading up to primary day in 2002, Norman's glorified gofer, Jeff Feldman, called to tell him the county organization needed $10,000 from Yellen for their efforts to get out the vote in central Brooklyn and Coney Island.

Levinson explained to Feldman that Yellen's campaign simply did not have that money and believed all along that county support meant that it would cover those last-minute expenses. Feldman made it clear, speaking as Norman's mouthpiece, that if Yellen did not deliver the $10,000, there would be no vital support on primary day. This kind of testimony might not have been new ground for the politically astute, but to hear it said under oath under the glare of the media spotlight was dramatic and damaging to the boss of Brooklyn politics. I came into the trial with extreme confidence and it grew by the day.

The testimony of Feldman, who took the stand as part of his agreement with us, supported what Levinson had said. (When Feldman agreed to be a witness, charges against him were dropped.) Norman's orders were, if she didn't come up with money, Yellen should be dumped; don't campaign for her, don't help her.

Yellen herself was the star witness as she recounted the meeting where Norman aggressively laid down the rules to her about whom she had to hire for campaign work and how much money she would have to fork over to county. Yellen, a trim woman wearing a red blazer and white blouse on the stand, clearly gained the jury's support as she explained her term as a civil court judge was up and she was fighting for reelection so she could continue her career.

Consistent with the testimony of Levinson and Feldman, Yellen described a series of three meetings in July 2002 during which Norman's rules were laid out to candidates. They began with demands that Yellen and Sikowitz come up with $100,000 to $150,000 to fund their campaigns, and the party would hire lawyers to defend their petitions if challenged.

In the beginning, Yellen said she had no problem with that amount of money but wanted to spend it how her advisers wanted to spend it, not how Norman demanded she spend it, and she did not want to be a part of a joint campaign with Sikowitz, a new candidate, and Robin Garson. Yellen felt her prior record of a decade as a judge—during which she wrote important decisions, received awards, and was endorsed by community leaders throughout Brooklyn—put her ahead of Sikowitz, who was running for the first time, and Garson, Gerald Garson's wife, who Yellen thought was just a party hack.

With these three running along with Judges Delores Thomas and Margarita Lopez Torres, it meant five women were running for three spots. Norman wanted Yellen, Sikowitz, and Garson as the party-endorsed ticket. Separating Yellen would make the other two look bad and drive voters to Thomas and Lopez Torres.

But from the first meeting on July 15, Feldman made it clear that the endorsed candidates would have to follow Norman's strategy and use his vendors, especially a favorite printer who stood to make big bucks on campaign material. Feldman threatened to withdraw support if they balked.

On July 23, with petition drives coming to an end, Feldman warned again that if their petitions were challenged, they would have to pay for their own campaign lawyers to fight the challenges if they had not yet agreed to use the printer. Also, now Feldman said Norman wanted $16,100 for a consultant, his friend William Boone III, whom he had chosen to help bring black voters to the polls. And Feldman told her Norman was firm on not distinguishing her from Sikowitz and Garson.

One week later the shit hit the fan. Yellen testified that tempers flared at a meeting and Norman revealed himself as an arrogant bully anxious to wield his power.

With Yellen at his side, Levinson was pushing Feldman hard for a definitive answer to what would be the penalty if they did not agree to the joint campaign. Feldman did not reply. So Levinson pushed harder. He turned to Norman, who until this point had not said a word. He asked Norman the same question: What would be the penalty?

Everyone waited on Norman's response. After a few seconds the county leader stood, slammed his hand on his desk, and declared, "We'll *dump* her."

Silence again. The boss had spoken. They had an agreement. Without county support, Yellen testified, she believed she could not win. She testified she would do anything possible to save her career.

But raising $9,000 to pay a printer Norman favored for handout materials and another $1,000 for primary-day consulting services of a Thurgood Marshall officer and close friend of Norman's was impossible. It never happened.

When Richardson asked her what she believed would happen when she could not pay, she turned to the jury, looked them in their faces, and with tears in her eyes said, "I would no longer be a judge. I would be out of a job." She was correct. It was as dramatic a moment as I had ever experienced in my career. Richardson handled it perfectly and let a few moments pass so the jury and everyone else in the courtroom could take it in before he resumed his questions.

In every trial you have moments when you feel that you have either hit the ball out of the park or have made an error with the bases loaded in the bottom of the ninth. When we finished with Yellen, I felt like we were winners. I did not know what Ricco and his partner in this trial, Edward Wilford, could do to reverse the tide. I thought we had proven Norman to be a greedy bully, anxious to demonstrate his power at any opportunity. That is what the case was about. It was not about race, as Ricco actually helped demonstrate as the trial continued.

As Richardson thanked Yellen and told the judge he was finished, I remember thinking that this long haul was coming to an end. There would be a few more witnesses from us, then the defense. But I thought the heavy lifting was over. Yellen provided that for me. She was a victim who told her story well.

On cross-examination of Yellen, Ricco failed to adjust his strategy and once again threw the race card on the table. He got Yellen to agree the $9,000 would be spent mostly on getting out votes in central Brooklyn's black neighborhoods. He suggested she was willing to spend money on white neighborhoods but not on black areas.

The argument went nowhere, but it did lead to one moment of levity in this otherwise very serious trial. Pointing out that the women whom the county had put up for the open civil court judgeships were all white and Jewish, Ricco, suggested that was proof that Clarence Norman was color-blind when it came to picking candidates to support.

But Yellen threw it right back at him. She answered that Norman could have run a multiethnic slate if he'd wanted, with her, Judge Delores Thomas, and Judge Margarita Lopez Torres. Ricco asked if Yellen's advisers believed it to be a waste of money for her to campaign for black votes "because Jewish people vote for Jewish candidates and black people vote for black candidates.

"But, when you went for chicken dinners in the African-American neighborhoods, did you say to those people, 'I'm here for your support' " and tell them "how good the chicken was?"

Yellen, now fully composed, looked at the jury and answered, "No, I didn't. Because the chicken wasn't that good."

Over the next week, testimony from Thomas and Lopez Torres further damaged Norman's reputation and made a farce out of the idea that he was a civil rights champion. Judge Delores J. Thomas testified that in 2002 Norman declined to support her run in the primary for civil court judge. She said that Norman told her he didn't think she had the right last name. Everyone in earshot took that to mean that Norman did not think a black woman could win that seat. His rejection of her was not the action of a civil rights warrior. It also made him look foolish as

Thomas found the resources to run without county's support and won anyway. Truly a victory for the people!

Lopez Torres testified that Norman refused to back her for a civil court spot because she would not hire the daughter of one of Norman's allies as her law secretary. Instead, Norman backed Robin Garson. She did not complain about using Norman's pals as consultants and letting Norman decide where to spend her money. With the county's support she ran uncontested and won. But so did Lopez Torres, who campaigned hard, raised her own money, and became a determined foe of Norman's and his way of running the party.

During summations, I had my chance to remind the jury how we'd delivered on our promise to provide evidence that Norman was guilty and how the defense failed to discredit that evidence.

The summation of a high-profile trial is of interest to the legal community as a whole. It is not unusual even for our colleagues from the office to crowd the gallery to hear the prosecution's closing argument. I have seen prosecutors save their cases with strong closings and have seen them blow the whole ball game as well.

My summation at the close of the second trial, when I quoted John Lennon's song, was still being talked about in the office. I received congratulations on it from even the most jaded prosecutors and a few defense attorneys not involved in the case. A professor friend of mine used it in his trial-advocacy class at St. John's law school. Even a couple of reporters, who had seen more trials than I had, complimented me on it. But as effective as it was, it would do me no good now. When you choose a jury, you ask if they have been following the case in the newspapers. Mostly, they are not aware of nuances and details reported in the press about a defendant's legal troubles. During this trial we were not allowed to reference Norman's previous convictions. My brilliant summation in the stolen-check trial would do me no good with this jury.

From the day I'd heard Ricco bring Martin Luther King Jr. into the case in his opening statement, I began planning how to turn that on him in my summation. After three weeks of sometimes riveting testimony I got my chance.

I reminded the jury of how important judges are to our everyday lives: "They are the cornerstones of our society. They preside over cases involving all races, creeds, nationalities, and make decisions every day that affect people's lives, livelihood, homes, marriages, and freedom."

I decried what we had learned over the length of the trial, of what judges had to go through in Brooklyn if they wanted to continue to be judges or become a judge. It was "nothing short of disturbing," I said. I told the jury that if you aspired to that lofty, honored position in Brooklyn, you had to go hat in hand to Clarence Norman, the political boss, the man who ran the machine. But he was a man, I said, who "does not care about qualifications." I took the jury through the demeaning process Lopez Torres and Thomas had had to overcome to fight for the opportunity to serve the people of Brooklyn.

To Clarence Norman Jr., Sikowitz and Yellen were easy marks, ripe for the picking in the rough-and-tumble world of

Brooklyn politics, and he could take advantage of them and enrich himself and enhance his power. I needed to challenge the idea of Norman as a great civil rights leader.

I was blunt: "Clarence Norman has been portrayed as a master strategist and compared to a great man and leader. I submit to you that the defendant is no better than the local tough guy who pretends to help the people in his community."

Then I came up with my own powerful quote. In his opening, I said, Mr. Ricco invoked the memory of Dr. Martin Luther King Jr. and compared the defendant to him. "Well, I'd like to quote Dr. King, who said, 'In societies on the pilgrimage toward democracy and the rule of law, no forms of intimidation are ever justifiable in the sight of God or humanity.' Apparently Clarence Norman never heard those words."

On February 23, 2007, Norman was convicted on charges of grand larceny and extortion. It was his third trial conviction in two years. As a result of his convictions he was forced to resign from his Assembly seat and had to give up his position as head of the Kings County Democrats. He was disbarred.

On April 17, 2007, Judge Marcus sentenced Norman to three terms of one-to-three years in prison to run consecutively for a total term of three to nine years, but allowed him to stay free on bail while his lawyers continued to appeal the first two convictions.

Then on June 5, 2007, his appeals exhausted, Norman appeared in a courtroom packed with his supporters, including his father, to hear Marcus's final words on the matter. Dressed as usual in a fine blue suit, Norman was stoic as Marcus said,

"Sentence is executed," then banged the gavel. Norman was handcuffed and led off to jail.

Norman's continuing denial of his situation was evident even at that moment. As he was being led off to the door that led to holding cells, where he would await the transfer to Rikers Island, Norman picked up a white paper bag that he had brought to court that morning. Before taking the fallen leader away, a court officer looked in the bag. He then took it away from Norman and handed it to a relative. Inside were cookies and a Walkman.

Chapter 10

Let's Go to the Videotape

The larger crimes are apt to be simpler, for the bigger the crime, the more obvious, as a rule, is the motive.

—ARTHUR CONAN DOYLE

FOR ALMOST THREE YEARS AFTER the Garson-related arrests, we were on a legal roller coaster. First, Judge Steven Fisher, the administrative judge of Queens County who was assigned to the case from the outset, dismissed six felony counts of receiving rewards for official misconduct. He saw those as violations of rules of judicial conduct, not criminal charges. He allowed the felony charge of bribe-receiving to stand as well as the misdemeanor charges of official misconduct and accepting unlawful gratuities. But our appellate team of Len Joblove and Seth Lieberman insisted from the get-go that the charges were solid and they would argue to get them reinstated. And that is what happened.

During the delays, Garson underwent cancer surgery, and Court Street rumormongers speculated he would not live to stand trial. But they were wrong. Periodically during the Norman trials even with everything else going on—the Mafia cops, the FBI guy under a cloud—hardly a day went by when I did not have to check in on the Garson developments. It was a constant presence in my office because it was a constant presence on Court Street and at every lawyers' social function. The Garsons were well-known. People were interested in what awaited them.

When Judge Fisher was promoted to Appelate Division judge, Jeffrey Berry, the administrative judge of upstate Orange County, was brought down to the city to oversee the Garson-related trials. He was a breath of fresh air. He wore a bow tie and had a folksy way about him, but he was no bumpkin. He had no ties to the Brooklyn political machine and was sharp as a tack. He knew the law and knew how to keep a trial moving along. He took no guff from anyone. I liked his style.

Shortly after the conclusion of the last Norman trial, Judge Berry called me and Garson's current lawyer, Ron Fischetti, to his chambers in Goshen, New York, the county seat of Orange County, where he usually presided, for a scheduling meeting and to float the idea of a plea deal for Garson. Driving up there with Brian Wallace, I realized how different that area was from Brooklyn. Farms and small villages with antiques stores still lined Route 17. I had no doubts Berry was the right man for this trial. He had proved it during the trials of Salerno, Sarnell, and Ellman.

I had not yet decided whether to put Frieda on the stand in the Garson case. I did not want her picked apart by the defense. I did not want her to lose her cool. And I was not sure the jury would relate to her: her looks and accent might turn them off. She had testified in the Salerno trial without problems, but I was still cautious.

During that trial she had an interesting exchange with Judge Berry. Her use of Brooklynese mixed with her Russian-Israeli accent caused the judge to stop her testimony on several occasions for clarification. On one occasion the unabashed Frieda replied, "Judge, you're not from Brooklyn, are you?" It broke the courtroom up and added to the legend of Frieda. Berry clearly empathized with her, not that it would affect his judgment.

Finally, the Garson trial began in Brooklyn Supreme Court, the very court where Garson once sat on the bench to administer justice. The trial lasted several weeks. The press eagerly awaited Frieda's appearance on the stand, but I ultimately decided not to use her. I did not want her personal animosity getting in the way of the facts. Sometimes when a victim is too emotional and hell-bent on revenge, the jury will find him or her less than credible. I had harbored similar concerns with Lawrence Watkins, Amy's father, but his testimony had been vital to the case.

I did not need Frieda. She had done her job. Instead, I had on the stand other women whose cases Garson had presided over. They were less dramatic than Frieda and got the job done in excellent fashion.

The case rested on the video and audio recordings. The trial was being held in one of the larger courtrooms in a relatively new courthouse, and it was equipped with the latest in audio/visual components. The jury saw every videotape recorded by our hidden camera in Garson's robing room and in the detective's duffel bag on huge flatscreens with excellent sound. It was a far cry from just a few years earlier when every trial employing video or sound recordings seemed to run into technical problems.

The jury saw tapes of Garson committing his crimes within the restaurants and, most important, accepting the cigars and that envelope full of cash. They saw him sing his song in honor of the cigar, and they saw him stuff $1,000 into his desk drawer, then ask to exchange it for a check for his wife's campaign.

Berry allowed cameras in the courtroom, not an automatic thing in the archaic courtrooms of New York State, and local television along with newspapers and radio gave the trial gavel-to-gavel coverage. Each night the humiliating videos we showed in the courtroom were repeated over and over on local and national news programs. Of course the jury was not supposed to be watching the news. But they had front-row seats every morning for the best show in town.

The national CBS magazine show *48 Hours* was also on the scene. The producer Patti Aronofsky became a fixture in the courthouse covering all the Garson-related cases, and the eventual show was the highest rated in the program's history. The story of the Garson investigation is continually broadcast on cable stations to this day.

As the trial proceeded, I could not shake from my mind the absurdity of Garson's not taking the plea deal that his lawyers were clearly pressing him to do.

One day while Garson was still wearing the wire trying to nab Clarence Norman, Garson, George Terra, and I were in his lawyer Kamins's office to discuss Garson's lack of progress. We needed him to get more aggressive. While the four of us were talking, Kamins's secretary stuck her head in to say he had a call he probably wanted to take in private. So, Kamins got up, left the office to take the call, and in a few minutes returned with a smile on his face, almost a laugh. "That was Victor Barron, calling from the prison yard up at Dannemora," he said. Garson turned green. I was holding back a huge laugh, and Kamins, a mischievous elf who always wore a bow tie, just looked at Garson, asking with his eyes, *Isn't it time to make a deal?*

But Garson continued to resist, fired Kamins, and then hired Fischetti, who was a high-profile defense attorney, one of the city's best, with many big wins in the federal courts under his belt.

Fischetti's defense was basically that a judge like Gerald Garson "was not going to throw away his robes for a hamburger." When he said that during a television interview with CBS reporter Lesley Stahl, he looked like he was holding back a laugh. Our investigation had determined that Siminovsky wined, dined, and influenced Garson to the tune of more than $10,000 spent in full view of the public in popular restaurants and bars. And the evidence proved that the more wining and dining Siminovsky showered on the judge, the more legal guardianships and therefore the more income Siminovsky received in return.

It was a good deal for Siminovsky. He was making a lot of money on his investment and with little concern about the women and children he was sworn to protect. Was this a case of thieves feeding off each other? Sure it was, and the only interest

I had in keeping Siminovsky on the street was to use him to snare a bigger fish.

Some in my own office did not agree with the strategy. They thought Siminovsky was as big a bum as Garson and we should have concentrated on sending him to jail for as long as possible and gotten Garson later. But I wanted both, and giving a break to Siminovsky served that purpose. He made those tapes possible.

Imagine, I thought, *what went on behind closed doors before we got our camera in that ceiling. That we will never discover.*

The media was filled with stories about Garson's alleged transgressions. To the public he was looking more and more like a crooked judge who hated women and had no respect for himself or his family.

Nissim Ellman also did a television interview, on the misguided advice of his lawyer, Gerald McMann, to counter all the negative publicity about the bribery network of him, Siminovsky, and Garson. In it he claimed he was only trying to help his community get good representation in court and that he did not even know Garson. He claimed he was just showing off, trying to be a big shot, when he showed Garson's phone number on his cellphone contact list to Frieda.

Later, on the robing-room hidden camera, Garson was caught on tape telling Siminovsky he had nothing to worry about in a case. Garson told Siminovsky to stop worrying that the wife in the case was going to lose her house and end up with nothing.

Then in a blatant disregard for lawyer-judge ethical standards, he instructed Siminovsky on how to present certain papers, regarding the deed to the couple's house, to the court and how to argue the case. I don't think I could have thought up any better scenarios to tape in the robing room if I had written the script.

Siminovsky performed the role of undercover cop better than Al Pacino ever had. If there were an Academy Award for Best Real-Life Presentation of an Informant, Paul Siminovsky would have won it hands down.

Of course it was all to serve his own purpose, to get himself out from under the jail sentence he was facing. But he eventually earned the respect of my entire team. He delivered what he promised: the evidence that Garson was a corrupt, woman-hating, arrogant crook who was stealing the public trust from the people.

Fischetti knew what he had signed up for, and once he got a look at all the evidence we had accumulated against Garson, he also argued for a plea deal to minimize the punishment Garson would face. Berry called us to his office for a second time to discuss a plea deal. He proposed that Garson plead guilty to two misdemeanors. Each would carry a penalty of a year in jail, and they would run consecutively. We figured he would spend about sixteen months behind bars. Berry also said he would arrange for Garson to serve that time in the Orange County jail, where he would be relatively close to his family and medical care.

I relayed the deal to Hynes, who said it would be okay with him. Garson was in his seventies, and thanks to the videos already released to the public and the testimony in previous trials, he had already become the butt of jokes. His career was over, and he was disgraced. The message to others who would try what he had done had been delivered. A longer prison sentence would not serve a greater purpose.

But again, Garson acted like he knew better than anyone else. After all, he was a supreme court judge. Who would know better about how to beat the system? He turned the offer down.

Hynes and I were shocked. What was he thinking? Fischetti did not want to go forward. So Garson hired his old friend Michael Washor, who agreed to go to trial and work for free. I thought Washor, while showing admirable loyalty, was not being a good friend if he was willing to participate in the further trashing of Garson.

The tapes were so stacked against him. They tarred him in other ways than just proving he was a criminal. His dancing around with the cigars and his constant disparagement of the women who appeared before him, including Frieda, were hard for anyone who had any measure of respect for our justice system to watch.

His favorite song, which he would sing to himself in the robing room, appeared to be "if you want to be happy for the rest of your life, never make a pretty woman your wife." He was caught on one robing-room tape making a sexual reference to Frieda Hanimov's lips. His wife, Robin, and his sons sat in the courtroom watching the spectacle as it was caught on our candid cameras and shown on two flatscreen television monitors.

I admired Robin's loyalty. She was also a tireless worker for the Brooklyn Democrats; that's how she got her judgeship. But now her reputation was also being bashed by a selfish husband. Gerald cared only about Gerald.

When I briefed DA Hynes on the progress of the case, he often expressed sympathy for the Garson family, but much more for the families like Frieda Hanimov's. He would remind us of his childhood in an abusive home and how his mother could not get satisfaction through the courts. Her complaints about her husband were often dismissed out of hand. Nothing changed for young Joe Hynes until as a teenager he physically threw his own father out of the house.

Washor added to the circus atmosphere of the trial. He had an outdated courtroom style, overtly trying to charm the jury and make them laugh like a borscht-belt comic. One reporter referred to him as the legendary Catskills comedian Shecky Greene.

He began by telling the jury it was his birthday, April 17. He said he had the honor on his birthday of summing up for someone he'd known for forty-eight years. He then turned dramatically toward his client and said, "This is for you, Gerry."

We at the prosecution table exchanged looks. We had never seen anything like it.

What happened one morning summed up the bizarre nature of the entire case, kind of put an exclamation point on it. As we were about to begin testimony, with the jurors in their seats, Washor suddenly remembered he had to make a phone call. He asked the judge for permission, saying he needed a minute to make the call. It was rude for him to do, but the tolerant Berry said it was okay with him.

Washor thanked the judge, then attempted to leap over the velvet rope that separates the gallery from the well of the courtroom where the lawyers and the judge are positioned. The portly Washor nimbly got one leg over the rope, then leaned his body into it and just about made it before his back foot caught and he went headfirst to the floor. As soon as everyone realized he was okay, the room burst out in laughter. I admit to joining in, but I felt sorry for the guy. Washor was not a bad guy. He was genial, likable, smart, and earnest, but Garson had handed him a lemon and no one could have made lemonade out of it.

In his summation, Washor reminded the jury that the trial was not about fixing cases. Technically, he was correct. Garson was never charged with fixing a case. We could not prove that he had. The charges were about giving preferential treatment to lawyers and manipulating the outcomes of divorce proceedings. We charged he received rewards for official misconduct. The tapes in the robing room, and the Archives bar at the Marriott, the Queen restaurant on Court Street, and Nino's near Garson's apartment in Manhattan, told the story better than we ever could. And Siminovsky said it himself on the witness stand.

Washor argued that before February 2003 there was no evidence that Siminovsky gave gifts, bought lunches, did favors for Garson. Well, that was true, our case began with the Siminovsky tapes. Washor claimed Ellman and Siminovsky were "pimping" Garson "without his knowledge." I kind of like that line. Washor was firing blanks but occasionally one would hit a target. But who believes a whore does not know what her pimp is doing?

The Garson team had no defense in the face of the videotapes. Still, like an ostrich putting his head in the sand, Washor just absurdly denied everything. For instance, Washor told the jury Garson never took money even though they saw it with their own eyes. And I made sure the jury saw that again when I played that segment of the tapes in my summation.

Washor tried to make Siminovsky the villain by saying he was a crooked lawyer who entrapped Garson to save his own skin. Well, yeah, whoever said anything different? Washor also tried to make Frieda out to be a hysterical nut who cared little about her children.

Of course he couldn't successfully do either because I had already told the jury in my opening statement that Siminovsky was crooked, but the tapes would show he was not a liar. And we kept Frieda off the stand so Washor could not insult her and get her to lose her cool in front of the jury—although, looking back, I think Frieda could easily have handled Washor. She was probably the smartest person involved in the entire case.

Still, as the jury was returning with their verdict, I heard Washor say to Garson, "We won." He was the only one in the courtroom who believed that. The verdict was guilty, and a few weeks later Judge Berry sentenced Garson to three and a third to ten years in prison.

That misdemeanor deal we'd offered earlier had to look good to him then.

Of the entire Garson cabal, only the court clerk escaped conviction.

For Frieda Hanimov, her daring, patience, and persistence paid off. With another judge presiding over her case, she was awarded full custody of all her children. In this case where justice seemed to have been perverted, actually it prevailed.

Chapter 11

Build Me a House . . . In Queens

You can't put the toothpaste back in the tube.

—H. R. Haldeman

TOWARD THE END OF the Norman cases, as if the Rackets Division did not have enough on its plate, the New York City Department of Investigation (DOI) brought a case. Brooklyn state assemblywoman Diane M. Gordon, Norman's political ally who took the Fifth when she might have defended him at his stolen-check trial, was allegedly seeking a bribe from a land developer.

The developer, who was facing jail time in an unrelated case in Nassau County, was trying to minimize some of his potential sentence by offering information on another crime. He went to the DOI, and an arrangement was made with Nassau County that would help him if he delivered. He was also hoping to avoid being snared in any investigation of Gordon's misdeeds. He apparently thought she would be caught.

DOI usually does its own investigations, but then turns its

conclusions over to an appropriate prosecuting agency for indictment and trials. But by the summer of 2004 my Rackets Division had proven so adept at investigating official corruption, they recognized we could be a big help, so they brought the CI to meet with me.

I was knee-deep in Norman, with Garson, Mafia cops, and former FBI agent DeVecchio still on my schedule, so I assigned Joseph DiBenedetto, a smart, diligent assistant district attorney, to work with DOI to see what they had and what we could do to help out. I asked the dependable Kevin Richardson to also keep on eye on developments.

With another Brooklyn politician in hot water, Hynes was all over us constantly for updates and offering strategy and legal advice. The political fallout, with Barron in Dannemora and Norman, Garson, and now Gordon heading for jail, could not be worse for him.

Hynes was performing a thankless service. His political allies were wary that he was getting too close to their own manipulations of the public trust, and his political enemies were now on a crusade to bring him down no matter how long it would take.

I knew I would go down with him if they were ever successful, but for the time being we all had a job to do. That was to enforce the law no matter where it took us. We did not talk about the eventual repercussions, but we were not children in the playground.

Gordon was a minor legend in Brooklyn political circles. She was a fifty-two-year-old native of South Carolina who'd graduated from New York Technical College and was a daycare worker before joining the staff of Assemblyman Edward Griffith, who took her under his wing. She was smart and ambitious, both valuable attributes for a career in politics. When she caught the attention of DOI, she was best known for running for office in 2002 against Griffith, who'd fired her after she took part in a demonstration against police brutality.

She got her revenge on Griffith by winning, but the people of Brooklyn turned out to be the losers. Gordon, who as a young community worker fought to help residents and businessmen fight off economic pressures that were forcing them out of their homes and neighborhoods, seemed to have lost her fire when she finally got in office and was an undistinguished performer in Albany. Apparently along the way she also lost her interest in fighting for those in need and decided to concentrate on the needs of Diane M. Gordon. She was overtaken by arrogance and greed.

The CI was a developer of vacant land that he would turn into middle-class homes. They were sorely needed in the parts of Brooklyn represented by Gordon, which contained two huge middle-class apartment building complexes. He told us that when he approached Gordon to ask her help in winning the rights to develop a city-owned parcel slated for public housing and worth about $2 million, she responded with a request of her own.

Gordon said she would be happy to help and had confidence she could deliver. After all, she had a track record of helping people improve their living conditions through a group she'd started called Save Our Homes. In return she demanded the CI build a home for her on a parcel he was developing, not in her district in Brooklyn, but in Ozone Park, Queens, just over the Brooklyn border. The home would be in a gated community and would cost $500,000. But she wanted it for free and knew how to cover her trail.

She proposed the CI take the mortgage from her. She would lay out some cash, but eventually he would forgive the mortgage. Then she would have a beautiful home in a gated community in an neighborhood far better than the one she represented in the State Assembly, all for virtually nothing. Gordon's seventy-two-year-old mother would be the intermediary for the exchange of money. In mob circles they would call her the bagman.

And there was more, the CI told us. Gordon also wanted him to spruce up her Brooklyn Assembly office. She wanted new doors, heavy, ornate wooden doors for the entrance into her private office. They cost $600 each. As one reporter pointed out, that was more than a month's rent in most of the apartments in Gordon's Assembly district.

Well, the DOI came to the right place. We decided that the best way to snare Gordon was via the same technique we'd used on Barron and Garson: get her on tape.

Once again George Terra and his crew stepped in, and sharing their expertise with the DOI detectives, he and his team wired up the CI and sent him off to get Gordon to repeat her demands while he wore a "button" camera in his shirt. It was smaller than the lipstick camera we'd hidden in Garson's ceiling, but for Gordon it was just as fatal.

The CI met with Gordon seven times, mostly in her office, and she built our case against her, laying out her demands, and exposing her avarice and disdain for her constituents. Also caught on the Gordon tapes during a meeting with the CI was a lawyer giving her advice on how to proceed with her illicit scheme.

DiBenedetto and Richardson and the DOI people were satisfied we had enough to indict Gordon. I joined them when they briefed the district attorney, and we decided to take what we had to a grand jury. An indictment including charges of bribe receiving, conspiracy, and official misconduct was quickly returned.

Before we made the indictment public, Hynes thought we should shake Gordon and see if she could help us toward our goal of uncovering more official misconduct. Gordon immediately agreed to see if she could gain some favor with us, and whoever the judge would be at her eventual sentencing. She faced at least six years in prison.

I was busy in the courtroom with Norman so DiBenedetto worked with Gordon as she approached certain politicians and tried to get them to give up their dirty secrets. This was when we were regularly getting tips about who else was dirty in Brooklyn. Gordon gave it the old college try, but she was not good at it. She was no Berenholtz or Siminovsky. She could not produce even though she told us she was certain about crooked dealings among colleagues she approached.

Part of her deal was to agree never to run again for public office. We kept her indictment under seal and her out of the public eye for about one year. But in early July she announced that she would seek reelection. Hynes hit the roof.

How arrogant could she be? She was facing six years in prison, and we had given her a long leash to try to help herself. She knew what was on the tapes. She saw her friend Clarence Norman Jr. go down. And she decided to break her promise, to go against her deal. Her arrogance overtook any rational thought she might have had.

As the Rackets Division became more involved in nailing Gordon, Noel Downey was also moving ahead with the investigation into the allegations that former FBI man DeVecchio had helped Gregory "Grim Reaper" Scarpa. Downey laid out the case for me in early 2006, and I took what we had to Hynes. He gave the okay to move forward with the grand jury, and in March DeVecchio was indicted on four murder charges for allegedly providing inside information to Scarpa, who then ordered the killings.

I would be prosecuting that trial personally, and I needed to begin preparation immediately. I brought Assistant District Attorney Michael Spanakos aboard the Gordon team to work with DiBenedetto.

Hynes told us to file the Gordon indictment we had been holding back while she tried to help us make other cases, and on July 10, 2006, we held a joint press conference with DOI commissioner Rose Gill Hearn on the nineteenth floor of our building. Every reporter in town showed up. We played some tapes that proved our case beyond a shadow of doubt.

On one tape Gordon warns the CI that he has to keep things

quiet: "Don't discuss this with your friends." Later she says, "I want these things [the land] delivered to you where I can get a home for little or nothing." But her most damaging statement came as she explains to the CI how to proceed and how careful they have to be. "If you want a dream to come true, you have to keep your mouth shut," she says.

Hynes ordered me to handle the arraignment, and that afternoon Gordon was released on her own recognizance. In the courthouse hallway following the arraignment, Gordon's lawyers were explaining that she had tried to back out of the deal with the CI and had no intention of following through. That is why she thought she could run for office.

John Noel, the late WNBC reporter, an insightful guy who knew Brooklyn politics, cornered me near the courthouse. He asked me to respond to her claim that she never intended to follow through. My practice was usually to respond to impromptu interviews with the same language I used when laying out the case for the judge. But a quote famously used by H. R. Haldeman when he was laying out crisis strategy to President Richard Nixon popped into my head. " 'You can't put the toothpaste back in the tube,' " I said. Noel laughed, and that was the sound bite on the news that evening.

Again a politician without a chance of beating the case rejected any plea deals, and in April 2008 the trial began. You might think that, just from reading about Barron and Garson, Gordon would have gotten the idea that a deal would benefit her. At least it would have saved her some measure of public humiliation.

Spanakos was the lead prosecutor at her trial, which was somewhat anticlimactic. The tapes recorded by the CI on our button camera had been made public over the past two years of legal wrangling, and Gordon did not enjoy community support equal to Norman's.

No charges of criminalizing politics were hurled at Hynes in this case. Gordon was not a political powerhouse, and her greed was too obviously on display in the tapes to argue she did not know what she was doing. She was convicted of third-degree bribe-receiving on April 8, 2008, and the following month was sentenced to two to six years in prison.

Commissioner Gill Hearn summed it up for all of us at a press conference: "As an elected official, Gordon was supposed to work for the best interests of her Brooklyn community. Instead, Gordon marketed herself as a corrupt legislator ready to use her position to help a private builder unlawfully acquire city-owned land in her district if he, in exchange, would build her a half-million-dollar house in a gated community in Queens for practically no money."

Chapter 12

Dealing with the Devil

If you lie down with dogs, you get up with fleas.

—Benjamin Franklin

In the spring of 2006, at a status conference on the DeVecchio case, Judge Gustin L. Reichbach raised the issue of the trial schedule. Reichbach was one of the more efficient judges serving in Brooklyn Supreme Court. He wanted to get things going.

But I was sick. I was feeling the effects of four demanding years of trials and investigations and the deteriorating health of my father and sister. I had forgone most vacation time and barely had a quiet weekend to spend time with my boys or even catch a Mets game on television.

The Rackets Division was clicking on all cylinders. Not all our cases were as high profile as the dirty judges and crooked politicians, but we were handling organized-crime murders, police brutality, money laundering, sex trafficking, and just about anything else you can find in the dictionary under crime. That is why I had wanted to be Rackets chief. I wanted a chance to get all the bad guys. So I got what I had asked for, but now my health was suffering as a result.

Speaking with difficulty, I explained to Reichbach that I had been diagnosed with severe bronchitis, and in addition to medication the doctors wanted me to get some rest. I was hoping to take a vacation at a villa my good friend the prominent lawyer Arthur Aidala had rented in Italy.

Reichbach knew I was not faking. He was well aware of the demanding schedule I had been following since 2002. I was hoping not to annoy him with my request to put the trial off until at least the fall. I thought we were lucky that Reichbach was assigned to this trial, and I wanted to keep him happy.

The efficient Reichbach came up with a solution based on the DeVecchio legal team's request for a Kastigar hearing to bar evidence. DeVecchio had two lawyers with a lot of experience in the federal courts, Douglas Grover and Mark Bederow. DeVecchio was a frequent witness in mob trials following the Colombo wars of the 1990s, which were mainly fought in Brooklyn. His testimony was key to putting away a number of mobsters. He was the head of the FBI's Colombo squad and had intimate knowledge of the family's dealings.

When he was called to testify at post-trial hearings, he wanted to take the Fifth. It seemed as if some of the things he had known and had not taken action on could possibly get him in hot water. It was not an unusual predicament for law enforcement officers who "handled" top-echelon gangsters like Gregory Scarpa. The agent was given "use and derivative immunity" for his testimony.

In the Kastigar hearing, the defense team of Bederow and Grover wanted to prove that our case, alleging DeVecchio gave tips to Scarpa that led to four killings, was based on testimony from those earlier federal hearings. They wanted the judge to bar us from using any information from that testimony or anything that derived from it as the basis for our case.

We had anticipated this, and I purposely ordered my DeVecchio investigators and prosecutors not to read any of that old testimony and not to follow any leads that might have originated in that testimony. Downey, our investigators, and I, barely able to speak at the time, had to swear to that during the Kastigar hearing. We swore under oath and in response to defense questions that our case was built on new evidence developed by us and presented to a grand jury.

We had one bump in the road when Downey admitted he collected copies of testimony in a hearing for mobster Vic Orena in 1997. Downey said he wanted them in the office in case they would be needed in any appellate situation following a DeVecchio conviction. He said he had it, but under oath said he had never read it and never discussed it with colleagues.

The media covered the hearings and got a preview of what road our trial strategy was to follow. It made big headlines, and as our efforts were disclosed to the public, tension grew between the US Attorney's staff, the FBI, and anyone connected with the Kings County District Attorney's Office.

Two former FBI agents were working as detectives for the defense. They, along with dozens of other supporters, showed up at every court appearance and jammed the courtroom gallery.

The courthouse hallway was lined with supporters forming a protective screen for DeVecchio, sixty-five, who was out on $100,000 bail, as he made his way to court. They tried to intimidate reporters whose stories they did not like. One reporter was even pushed around in the hallway after exiting the courtroom. Inside the courtroom they sat stone-faced, glaring at me and my team as we argued our case. Their tactics were similar to those of gangbangers, from the Crips and the Bloods and other Brooklyn street gangs, who would show up when a member was on trial and make nasty faces at cops, witnesses, prosecutors, judges, jurors, and court officers. It would be funny if the stakes were not so high. The only friends we were making were among the families of Scarpa's victims and some former colleagues of DeVecchio's who thought he had crossed the line.

I had been pleased with the appointment of Reichbach to the case because he had a history of social activism and challenging the government. We did not want a judge who would stand behind the FBI no matter what evidence we presented that the agent broke the law.

Reichbach was a student-protest leader at Columbia University in the sixties. As a lawyer he fought for housing rights, and he later served on a war-crimes tribunal in Kosovo. He decorated his courtroom with a neonlit scales of justice and pictures of Clarence Darrow and Paul Robeson. He would not be intimidated by DeVecchio or his FBI friends who would pack the gallery. He might have been a product of the Democratic Party clubhouse, but he was one they got right. He had a lot of admirers in the DA's office.

He ruled in our favor in the Kastigar hearing, and trial was scheduled for the fall. I was able to take a breather. I got some rest at home, spent some days at Jones Beach, a favorite getaway spot for me since childhood, and then flew off to Italy with Artie and his family and a few other friends.

But I never got DeVecchio off my mind. It was too big a deal. In a sense it was bigger than Norman. We weren't dealing with stealing money. We were dealing with murder.

From the first day I had any conscious thought about bringing DeVecchio to trial, I'd thought about cross-examining him on the stand. I figured his lawyers would want him to testify.

He was charismatic, smart, impressive. Tall, good-looking, well-spoken, he was just what you would want an FBI agent to look and sound like. He had an admirable record in law enforcement. If I were his defense attorney, I would put him on the stand.

This guy was no Clarence Norman Jr. As dramatic as my confrontations with Norman were, any clash with DeVecchio would be epic. He had street smarts honed by years of manipulating and deceiving shrewd mobsters who lived by their wits. This head-to-head, no-quarter-given struggle would be remembered for a long time.

So I was constantly preparing for that confrontation. I researched his career. I spoke to law enforcement officials who'd worked with him, especially some NYPD organized-crime detectives. I learned some admired him on one hand as a handler of a high-echelon Mafia figure, and for the same reason some wondered whether he was too cozy with Scarpa.

Some of his fellow agents felt the same way, and I planned to have them testify. Also on the stand for the prosecution would be former members of Scarpa's crew who suspected an irregular relationship with an FBI agent.

But the star witness for the prosecution would be Linda Schiro, Scarpa's longtime mistress, who was at his side through his mob career and his days as an FBI informant, which went back to the 1960s. She knew DeVecchio and had a lot to say about his influence on her common-law husband and vice versa.

Our case against DeVecchio was met with skepticism from the day we announced the indictment to the day testimony began. DeVecchio was known to crime reporters who had covered the Colombo wars as well as those who regularly reported on the US Attorney's Office and the FBI. That group understood what was going on during that chaotic period and understood that rules got broken and strange alliances were formed.

The Colombo family war broke out after the boss, Carmine Persico, who was in prison, named underboss Vic Orena as acting head. But in this half-assed anointment, Persico made it clear that when his son Allie Boy finished his own prison stint, he would become boss.

Orena went along with the plan for a while, but once he got a taste of being boss, he decided he would never give it up. Instead he plotted to kill Allie Boy. The assassin would be "Wild Bill" Cutulo. In 1976 as a green assistant district attorney I prosecuted Wild Bill three times for murder. The first trial ended in a hung jury. We later developed evidence that a juror had been paid off to vote for acquittal. The second trial also resulted in a hung jury, and he was outright acquitted in the third trial. It is not easy to convict a wiseguy in Brooklyn.

The murders DeVecchio was indicted for all had to do with suspected informants in the Colombo family and "Grim Reaper" Scarpa in particular. Scarpa worked on Persico's side. Scarpa was dying of AIDS, but it did not stop him from doing his job, which was to go "hunting" on the streets of Bensonhurst and gun down any Orena-faction members who fell into his sights.

That was his day job, so to speak. His part-time job was to inform on the very men he worked alongside with as a killer, burglar, loan shark, bookie, and all-around enforcer. The man he informed to, with the blessing of the FBI, was DeVecchio, his handler. That was never in dispute. The question was, did DeVecchio ever help Scarpa do his day job?

To my surprise, DeVecchio waived his right to a jury trial. He would put his fate in the hands of Reichbach. I am not sure why he decided that. Perhaps it was to remove emotion from the case, to make the case rise or fall strictly on the law. A judge would not let his personal feelings, his love or hate of the FBI, for instance, get in the way of the verdict. The decision showed he had a lot of respect for Reichbach even in light of the judge's antigovernment history.

The trial moved along according to my plan. I tracked down Carmine Sessa, consigliere to the Persico faction, who was in the witness protection program. He testified about Scarpa's legendary luck in not being arrested for the many small crimes he carried out, such as jewel robberies. But he believed the FBI would never let him get away with murders even if he was a top-echelon informant.

I put Larry Mazza, Scarpa's protégé, on the stand. He described Scarpa as a fearless desperado who was totally unconcerned about getting caught. He said the crew suspected their boss had some sort of protection. They believed he had someone on the take, someone he referred to as "the girlfriend."

After a couple of days of testimony, the DA's press spokesman told me the reporters were starting to come around. That they were getting the picture, their skepticism was turning to belief.

All awaited the testimony of Linda Schiro, Scarpa's mistress of forty years, who was at his side from his early days as an FBI informant when he went to Mississippi to help solve the murders of three civil rights workers, until the Grim Reaper himself met his end. The couple never legally married but had a son and a daughter together.

Linda, now in her sixties, still showed some of the beauty she was when she first hooked up with Scarpa. But a lifetime of drugs and alcohol had taken its toll. My colleagues worried about putting her on the stand. Her life with Scarpa was tumultuous from the beginning. She would never be mistaken for a Sunday-school teacher.

But we worked hard at preparing her. We wanted her to tell all she knew about the Scarpa-DeVecchio relationship. We wanted her to be calm, careful, and unemotional. She did a good job.

She told the court how DeVecchio was a regular visitor to their home. She said she saw Scarpa give DeVecchio money and gifts of stolen goods, and she said she heard DeVecchio give Scarpa information about some eventual victims. She confirmed that Scarpa was paid by the government for his services.

Linda held up fairly well on cross-examination. She was asked about her drug use and her alcohol problem. Grover, however, did punch some holes in her testimony and exposed some inconsistencies, trying to make her sound like a liar. But overall, I thought our star witness won the day. I was confident I could patch up the holes on redirect examination the next day. I still looked forward to the possibility of getting DeVecchio on the stand. Surely, now, I thought, they would have to put him on to counter what Mazza and Schiro had sworn to.

Then it all came down around me.

As I was gathering my notes and other documents, stuffing them into my busting-at-the-seams briefcase, someone reached across the velvet rope that separated the lawyers from the gallery and tapped me on the shoulder.

I turned around to see a young, well-dressed man who introduced himself to me as Zach Margulis-Ohnuma, a lawyer for the *Village Voice* newspaper. He said, "Mike, the *Voice* has a story online right now about this case that I think you would want to see." He said it might effect how I proceeded with the trial.

I had no doubt he was legitimate, although this case had attracted a group of oddball characters—some reporters with their own agendas, freelance investigators, and an author or two, all of whom had their own theories on the myriad entanglements of the FBI. But I just knew this guy was not one of them. He was courteous, professional, and confident.

Our press spokesman was still in the courtroom and I asked him if he knew anything about a breaking story in the *Village Voice*. He said he would check into it, and before I got back to my office, he called me and said he'd found the story and suggested I read it as soon as possible. I got on the computer in my office.

The *Voice* had a story online about one of their reporters, the highly regarded Tom Robbins. Ten years earlier while doing research for a book on Scarpa with reporter Jerry Capeci, who specialized in writing about organized crime, Robbins interviewed Linda Schiro. They taped the interview session, and Robbins had recently discovered the tape in an old shoebox in the bottom of a closet. On the tape in response to questions from Robbins and Capeci, Linda pretty much contradicted what she had told us during our investigation and what she had just testified to in court.

I put in a call to the DA, then went up to the press office to see what reaction the story was getting from the rest of the media. Their phones were ringing off the hook. Everyone was asking for a reaction and what we planned on doing with the case. For the time being, we answered that we were looking into the story.

District Attorney Hynes reached me in the press office. I told him what the story said. I told him how it shot down all the useful testimony we got from Linda that day. But I reminded him that she was under oath in the courtroom, not in the interview ten years earlier. He got my meaning and asked what I wanted to do.

I said I did not want to do anything until I heard the tapes for myself. He agreed and told me to arrange to listen to the actual recordings. The *Village Voice* lawyer, Margulis-Ohnuma, arranged for Tom Robbins to bring the tapes to my office the following day.

The next morning as I approached the courthouse, the impact of the story was clearly evident. Jay Street between the DA's office building and the courthouse was lined on both sides by news trucks. Reporters were reporting live from the scene about the blockbuster development that might sink the trial against former FBI agent Roy Lindley DeVecchio.

I negotiated my way through the gaggle of reporters and up to Reichbach's courtroom. The DA did not want me to hide from the media, but we agreed with our press officer that it would not be wise to speak publicly until after we explained to the judge what we intended to do.

The courtroom was packed wall to wall. DeVecchio's crew filled the gallery. Many of my colleagues also showed up to show support for the district attorney.

I stood in front of Reichbach and brought him up to speed on what had transpired since yesterday's session. He had read and heard the news accounts, but what I said was on the record, and that's all he would have to consider. The only sworn testimony Linda Schiro had ever given about the relationship between her lover and DeVecchio was what she had said on the witness stand the day before. But the judge would have to consider the published reports about her earlier statements as well.

I told the judge that in light of the emergence of the tapes from the shoebox in the closet, I was requesting a twenty-four-hour adjournment so I could listen to the tapes before making a decision about the trial. The defense, now gleeful that their client might he saved, agreed. Reichbach ordered us to return the next morning.

Later that morning in my conference room, my team, including Kevin Richardson, Jackie Linares, and Laura Neubauer, along with Bederow, Robbins, and the *Voice* lawyer, listened to the ten-year-old tapes. I listened to the tapes with an open mind. I knew Linda was abusing drugs at the time of the interview. I knew she was also drinking heavily. As the tapes played, I could hear the clinking of glasses and wondered whether she was drinking during the interview.

But I also heard her answer the direct question of whether DeVecchio was giving information to the Grim Reaper that might have led to murders. She vehemently denied that. She contradicted what she had told my investigators, what she had told me, what she had told the grand jury, and what she had testified to over the prior two days.

I knew we could not go forward. Reichbach would surely allow the defense to bring the tapes into evidence. Linda's credibility and our case were shot to hell.

I went up to the press office to prepare them for calls they would get when the defense leaked what they had heard to reporters, and I called Hynes with the bad news.

After I filled him in, but without offering a suggestion on how to proceed, he asked me one question: "If you knew about these tapes before the trial, would you have gone ahead with it?"

That was a question I had been asking myself for the past two days. The answer was no. I would not have. Our case was based on the testimony of Linda. Even with a sympathetic jury I could not overcome this taped evidence. And this case was not being heard by a jury, but by a smart, careful judge.

Although I did have her daughter, "Little Linda," to corroborate some of her testimony, I understood going forward from here would be pointless.

Hynes ordered me to dismiss the case the next morning.

I was a little surprised at Hynes's quick reaction. I somewhat expected him to fight on. He usually had a stubborn streak about defending his cases.

I have wondered for years about his decision. He was correct; we could not have convicted DeVecchio without Linda, but you don't win them all. The important thing is to pursue justice for the victims, and I firmly believed we were doing that. However, the defendant also deserves justice and the protection of the law. Our obligation was to conduct a fair trial. I have no argument with that.

Friends of mine over the years, even law enforcement people on all levels and some journalists, have suggested to me that Hynes was caving to pressure from the highest levels of the Justice Department who did not want this trial to go forward in the first place. The government was still feeling humiliated and disgraced by the case in Boston where FBI agent John Connolly was sent to prison for helping the man he "handled," the notorious Whitey Bulger, commit crimes. But either way, my task was now to explain to the judge that we were bailing out.

That evening, alone in my office, I wrote the statement I would make the next day. It was the most difficult thing I ever had to do in a courtroom.

In the morning I went back in front of the bench where Reichbach sat and said, "Had we been provided with these tapes much earlier in the process, I dare say we would not have been here. The interest of justice at this point requires me to stand before you and ask you on behalf of the district attorney to dismiss or accept the dismissal of this indictment."

Grover said he did not object, and the courtroom broke out in cheers as DeVecchio's lemmings celebrated.

But Reichbach had not yet banged the gavel, and before he did, the court officers demanded the courtroom calm down, and then Reichbach surprised us all. People settled quietly into their seats and listened as he delivered a statement of his own, something he must have spent the entire previous day working on. I was flabbergasted by its direct blast at the FBI and its complimentary tone toward the district attorney. The dismissal meant that the trial record would be sealed, but the judge had the last word, and it was reprinted in a publication for lawyers and is available to the world today on the Internet.

He began with a nineteenth-century quote from Friedrich Nietzsche that "he who fights with monsters might take care lest he thereby become a monster . . . and if you gaze into the abyss, the abyss gazes also into you."

Reichbach said he felt "obliged to make some observations based on the testimony and exhibits revealed to date." He said that what had been introduced as evidence, "particularly by the defendant's own colleagues, is directed not so much to defendant's actions but to the institutional questions raised by the evidence."

The judge pointed to the testimony of former consigliere Carmine Sessa, who testified that Scarpa's crew had trouble believing that Scarpa was an FBI informant because they would not employ "a murderer as vicious and prolific as Greg Scarpa." Reichbach reminded us that Scarpa was such a lowlife that he even informed on his own son Greg Scarpa Jr. and that "in keeping with his own treacherous nature, he also provided information to the FBI that was purposely deceptive and untrue in an attempt to point the finger of accusation away from his own misdeeds and on to that of gang rivals."

Reichbach said it was impossible to determine how much of Scarpa's information was accurate, but it was "undeniable . . . that in the face of the obvious menance posed by organized crime, the FBI was willing, despite its own formal regulations to the contrary, to make their own deal with devil."

The FBI, he wrote, shielded Scarpa with immunity for fifteen years. He said the record indicated the FBI shielded Scarpa from "prosecution for his own crimes. . . . That a thug like Scarpa would be employed by the federal government to beat witnesses and threaten them at gunpoint to obtain information regarding the deaths of civil rights workers in the South in the early 1960s is a shocking demonstration of the government's unacceptable willingness to employ criminality to fight crime."

Reichbach also compared the government's coziness with the likes of Scarpa to the use of torture on suspected terrorists to get information: "These are shortcuts that devalue legitimate police work, their yield is insignificant and the cost to the fundamental values they debase is enormous."

As the packed courtroom sat in silence, reporters writing frantically trying to get Reichbach's every word, I stood at the prosecution table, filling with satisfaction that we were at least successful in helping to reveal the dangerous alliances the FBI made before and during the Colombo war. Reichbach continued with a mention of one of my witnesses, Detective Sergeant Fred Santoro, who said in dealing with informants—he called them "scum of the earth"—you had to assume they were lying. Then Reichbach singled out for praise "Special Agents Favo, Tomlinson, and Andjich," whom I had put on the stand: "In the face of what must have been enormous institutional pressure to turn a blind eye when they grew increasingly concerned that the defendant had lost the necessary perspective and had grown too close to his informant, they stepped forward, risking the opprobrium of their colleagues."

Reichbach stated that there was no evidence, save the discredited testimony of Linda Schiro, that DeVecchio committed any of the acts charged in the indictment. "On the other hand, credible evidence was presented that indicated that the defendant was so eager to maintain Scarpa as an informant that he was willing to bend the rules, including sending misinformation to headquarters."

Reichbach continued, "A top-echelon informant, that is a made member of organized crime who is willing to provide valuable intelligence, presents a difficult challenge to those who are sworn to fight crime. It is the inescapable aporia of law enforcement that they must sometimes turn a blind eye to criminality in order to prevent or combat greater criminality. It is a difficult balancing act but one this Court is forced to conclude, the Bureau failed miserably to accomplish in their dealings with Greg Scarpa."

I took a small measure of satisfaction in what Reichbach said next: "I have great respect for the District Attorney's office to dismiss this prosecution in the face of the contradictions between the testimony here at trial of their chief witness with the statements she's made previously on the matters in issue." He never said the prosecution was misguided from the beginning. He concluded by agreeing with the DA's decision and ordered the case dismissed.

A few years later in an interview with Anderson Cooper on *60 Minutes,* DeVecchio confirmed Reichbach's conclusion about his relationship with Scarpa. Cooper asked DeVecchio if he knew that Scarpa was killing people during the time DeVecchio was "handling" him during the Colombo war of 1991.

DeVecchio answered, "Yes, that's correct."

Cooper followed up, "And did you know it at the time?"

"Sure, I knew it because that's the guy he was."

Despite the serious tone of Reichbach's statement, when he

finished, it was like a New Year's Eve celebration in the courtroom with the lemmings congratulating each other and reaching out to shake DeVecchio's hand and pat him on the back.

Bederow and Grover said some unflattering things about me, and the district attorney and I kept to our strategy of not hiding from the media as I made myself available in the courthouse hallway. I stuck to what I said in front of Reichbach, and after a few minutes the reporters went off to chase Linda and members of the victims' families.

A *Daily News* reporter caught up with Linda's daughter, Little Linda, outside on Jay Street. She defended Linda, telling the reporter, DeVecchio "got away with murder."

And Mary Lampasi, a daughter of one of the murder victims, said she did not believe justice was served. "I know there are a lot of other things Linda Schiro is not talking about," she told the *News.*

For his part, in an incredible display of arrogance, DeVecchio ate a celebratory dinner that night in Sparks Steak House, the site of the rubout of mob kingpin Paul Castellano, which paved the way for John Gotti's emergence as the boss of much of New York's Mafia.

Chapter 13
A Visit with Lucifer

Go to heaven for the climate, hell for the company.
—Mark Twain

After the dust settled on the DeVecchio case, one piece of unfinished business still remained. When we were first prepping for the trial, we thought it would be a good idea to have Greg Scarpa Jr. in New York so we could question him about the relationship between his father, the Grim Reaper, and the FBI agent.

He was doing forty years to life for a drug conspiracy in the nation's toughest maximum-security prison, called Admax, in Florence, Colorado. So about a year before the trial was set to begin I sent detectives to bring him back here. With the cooperation of the Federal Bureau of Prisons, he would be held in the Metropolitan Correctional Center in lower Manhattan, just across the Brooklyn Bridge from our offices in downtown Brooklyn. We could bring him to Brooklyn for questioning.

Pat Lanigan, one of the detectives who brought Scarpa here

from Colorado, said he was agreeable and cooperative, and emotional about being out in the world again after being held in the isolation of maximum security for so many years.

Lanigan said that the killer almost broke down in tears as they walked through the Denver airport and he saw how the world had changed so much while he was behind bars. He had never before seen cell phones in operation. Lanigan is a tough guy and no one was feeling sorry for Scarpa, a vicious mobster, but you do get to observe a range of human emotions in this business.

His escorts were most touched by Scarpa's yearning for a Coke. He said he had not had a soda in more than a decade and it was one of the things he missed most. Before they arrived in New York, they made sure Scarpa got his soda.

We allowed Scarpa to meet with his family and brought in some of his favorite Italian food when we had him in Brooklyn for questioning. We needed his cooperation. We wanted him happy. We wanted him to tell the truth.

We never used him on the witness stand because the case was dismissed, and we returned him to federal custody. But one thing that he said to me when he first came to Brooklyn had stuck in my mind. He told us that in prison he was in a cell between the infamous Gaspipe Casso and John Gotti's right-hand man, Sammy "the Bull" Gravano. They could communicate by using the cardboard inserts from toilet-paper rolls to blow out the water in the drains in their sinks. When the pipes were clear of water, the neighbors could talk to each other, just like soccer moms gossiping over a picket fence. When Scarpa told

Casso he was going to New York to be grilled by me, Casso asked him to deliver a message: "Tell him I want to speak with him."

Casso last had my attention during the Mafia cops case, but that was almost ancient history with the two bum detectives rotting away in prison. At that time his lawyer had said he would not speak to me unless the Feds granted him immunity, which they refused to do. I didn't understand it then as he was already serving seventeen life sentences plus 450 years.

But I had not forgotten what Scarpa had told me. So I called the US Attorney's Office and asked for permission to speak to Casso, who was now in a prison hospital in North Carolina battling prostate cancer. They had no problem with my speaking with him if I promised not to discuss the Mafia cops case. They did not want him telling me anything that I would be forced to act on and possibly upset that apple cart. I totally understood their position and readily agreed. I was not looking for more agita with the US Attorney.

I wanted Chief Investigator Joe Ponzi and the ubiquitous George Terra along with me—not only as witnesses to what Casso had to tell me, but also because I knew their inquiring minds might pick up on something I would overlook. Ponzi was a renowned expert in the use of lie detectors, which made him adept at recognizing nuances, and small hints in responses to questions that the average person would miss.

Ponzi and Terra together were a walking, talking encyclopedia of Brooklyn mob crime from the 1970s to the present. Casso had asked specifically to talk to me, but I did not think he would mind Ponzi and Terra listening in. I had learned over the years that people incarcerated for a long time enjoy the attention they get when they tell their stories and reveal dark secrets. When they are helpful, they like to think of themselves as one of the guys, a part of the team.

In reality, we never fully trust them, and I know they never fully trust us. A life in law enforcement, no matter which side you are on, teaches you to be wary of everyone. Even cops and prosecutors have their agendas, and it is rare when they are compatible.

I did not hold out high hopes that Casso would lead us to the body of Jimmy Hoffa or anything like that, but I wanted to meet him. Organized crime falls under the umbrella of the Rackets Division, and Casso was one of the most notorious Brooklyn organized-crime figures since Murder Incorporated left its trail of blood from Canarsie to Coney Island.

Since the early 1960s when Joe Valachi sung to a congressional panel about a secret society called Cosa Nostra, organized crime has mostly been the purview of federal law enforcement. Their powers to pursue conspiracies and crimes across state borders make prosecutions more efficient. We gave up the Mafia cops case to the Feds partly because they were subjects of a Drug Enforcement Administration investigation at the same time we were pursuing them for being hired guns to the Brooklyn mob. In fact, they were finally arrested by DEA agents in Las Vegas.

In Rackets, most of our organized crime cases involved gambling, money laundering, and loan-sharking, and in recent years prostitution rings. Deputy District Attorney Chris Blank was our expert on organized crime and had an excellent working relationship with the US Attorney's Office and FBI.

One thing the Rackets Division did do each year, on Super Bowl Sunday, was raid bookie joints. Our undercover detectives would place bets in the illegal joints sometime during the week, thus giving us the legal reason to barge in on Sunday and clean the places out. That was historically the busiest day of the year for illegal betting, and the national take could be around a billion dollars. We called the annual operation Kings Flush.

We would have a press conference following the raids, announcing how many bookies we'd arrested and how much in betting slips we'd confiscated. DA Hynes would use the occasion to rail against illegal betting, which he called a cash cow for organized crime. Each year he would call for the state legislature to legalize sports betting as a way of ridding it from the influence of mobsters and reducing their illicit incomes as well.

Over the past decade, the Kings Flush raids had become less and less meaningful as organized bookies moved their operations offshore, to Caribbean islands, and the betting was conducted over computers. It's difficult to arrest the Internet.

But I also had another motive to meet Casso. I was an adjunct professor at St. John's University's College of Professional Studies, where I taught a class on the history of organized crime. I have also taught classes on trial advocacy at various law schools, but it was the organized-crime classes that the students loved best. They always sat transfixed as I related the history of the Mafia, from its roots in Sicily to its dominance of all criminal activities in the United States.

Many times I would sit with prosecutors and investigators in my office discussing an organized-crime case, then rush off to Jamaica, Queens, to lecture the students. I always made them extremely aware that with rare exceptions, such as Lucky Luciano or Meyer Lansky, the bosses of organized crime bled to death in the street or died alone in prison. Casso was heading for the latter.

Driving from the airport to the prison in Butner, North Carolina, was a new experience for me. I had never before been in that part of the country, but a few minutes on the road and I saw what people loved about it. When we'd retrieved our luggage in the airport, I'd noticed a lot of travelers with golf bags. Now I saw why. It seemed like every quarter mile or so there was another golf course. It was a far cry from Brooklyn! I'd never had much time for golf in my life, especially not in the past six years since the Barron investigation. I vowed to someday take it up just so I could enjoy the atmosphere. I'm a beach guy, but I soaked in the green grass and trees and calming atmosphere of the area. I wondered how inmates on their way to the various facilities at Butner felt about leaving this paradise and heading behind bars.

The Bureau of Prisons could not have been more helpful to us. They arranged for us to meet Casso on a day that was not a regular visiting day. So, when we were brought to the large visitors' room, it was totally empty except for us three guys from Brooklyn. We stood in an awkward semicircle waiting for Casso.

After a few minutes the killer was brought in. Because I'd heard his name so many times over the years and details of his crimes, I felt like I knew him. But I had never met him before that day. My first impression was surprise at how short he was. I expected he might look sickly from his prostate cancer, and although he looked older than his age, he did not appear ill.

I taught that the mob ran on the patron/client system. The patron always took care of his clients, who in turn made sure he was taken care of. Casso was a particularly paranoid patron.

Most mob bosses were not worldly men. They ruled over small pieces of territory, usually the neighborhoods they grew up in, and were wary of anyone who worked for them that was not geographically close. The most notorious mob rubout caused by this paranoia was when the New York mob killed Bugsy Siegel, whom they had sent out to Las Vegas to open what would become the Flamingo Hotel and Casino. After a while they felt they could not control their "client" and he was murdered.

Casso did something similar. He had a small crew working for him in Pennsylvania, and no matter how much money they delivered to his Bensonhurst headquarters, he grew more and more distrustful of them. One day he and a lieutenant drove out to Pennsylvania supposedly to parley with the crew, just a few guys, but really to murder them. They gunned them down as they arrived for the meeting.

That is the kind of thing I was thinking about as we stood around for a minute or two while the guard removed Casso's handcuffs and walked out. We had previously been told that someone would be looking in at all times, and that we could each only take a pencil and paper in with us.

So there we were, three lawmen and a killer serving seventeen life sentences, alone waiting to talk about murders. The scene reminded me of a time, years ago, when I was in private practice when I was interviewing a client in the Metropolitan Correctional Center in Manhattan. The two of us sat alone in a huge room that had one wall of windows looking out onto a hallway. Halfway into our discussion, a bell started ringing and the venetian blinds on the windows were drawn shut. Now we were sitting in a fairly dark room and could hear people making a commotion somewhere else in the building, but no one told us anything.

It was the first time I was meeting this client. When I gave him a questioning look, he just shrugged his shoulders. He had no idea what was going on either. So we sat there and I continued my questioning. We sat for what felt like three hours, then finally the venetian blinds were opened and a guard came in to take my client away.

At last, I was told I could leave the room and I made my way to the bank of elevators, where a crowd was waiting to leave the building. I was not the only one trapped. I later learned that we got caught in a lockdown because the guards were "moving the rats"—taking stool pigeons from one part of the prison to another.

I pushed myself into an already-jammed elevator and we began the journey down. No sooner did we start down than the elevator stopped at a lower floor. The doors opened and there stood the "Dapper Don," John Gotti, wearing an orange prison jumpsuit. He clearly could not fit in the jammed elevator car. He just said, "Hiya, fellas," and stood there as the doors closed. The encounter made a weird day even weirder.

I relived that day as I stood across from Casso as Ponzi and Terra introduced themselves and shook hands with the onetime underboss boss of the Lucchese crime family. As I started to introduce myself, Casso held up a hand. "I know who you are, Mike, half the guys in this place have your picture on the wall and throw darts at it."

I knew that was not true, but I took it as a compliment coming from a guy like Casso. I took it as that he respected me and the work I did.

To break the ice, I asked him if he had read *Friends of the Family,* my book about the Mafia cops case, in which his gang is featured prominently. He said he did. "It was about ninety percent accurate," he said. I took that as another compliment.

We then went to a small conference room we were told we could use, and we sat down. "Before we start, "I said, "I want to tell you than we cannot talk about the Mafia cops case. I don't want to hear anything you have to say about them." Casso responded that he understood. He was a street-smart guy. I did not have to explain further.

However, I could not resist reminding him that at one time I wanted to talk about them, but he refused to see me because the Feds would not give him immunity for his testimony, even though he was already serving seventeen life sentences.

His response to that surprised me: "That was my lawyer's idea. I was fine with seeing you, he didn't check with me."

Reluctantly, I knew I had to move off that discussion and

asked him why he wanted to see me now. He said he had information on unsolved murders that he could share with us. In return for his help, he wanted a letter to his judge that might help him get a reduction in his sentence.

Greg Scarpa Jr. wanted the same thing from us, and he might have benefited from it. He was facing a minimum of forty years, but that could be reduced. I wondered why Casso thought such a letter would be helpful to him. If you are serving seventeen life sentences plus 450 years, does it make you feel better to knock the score down to sixteen? Does that provide some hope that you may someday walk free? That is hard to imagine if you are not in such circumstances. Who knows how criminals look at life as they spend decades behind bars with no hope of release.

I told him we were interested in anything he had to say that would help us solve crimes. But I pointed out that anything he told us would have to be corroborated by hard evidence or at the least the sworn testimony of someone else. He understood that.

The Bureau of Prisons said we could have four hours with Casso, and we used up almost all of it as he gave us a guided tour of where bodies were buried in Brooklyn. He even drew us a map of a spot in Sheepshead Bay where he dumped a gun he used in a murder.

I promised him would we check out every lead he gave us. Ponzi and Terra took notes. From time to time their expressions revealed they knew which cases Casso was talking about.

Before we ended our session, I broke the promise I made to

the US Attorney about discussing the Mafia cops case. I asked Casso if he would tell us where Jimmy Hydell's body was buried. The investigation of Hydell's disappearance was what had eventually led to the arrest and conviction of the rogue cops.

Casso told us a friend of his was operating a bulldozer on land being cleared for a housing development. He said he dumped the body in front of the dozer's blade, and his friend made sure it was buried deep under the foundation.

We all knew there would be no chance of recovering it, but back in Brooklyn I passed on the information to Hydell's mother. I hope it gave her some closure.

With that we said good-bye to Casso, promising to report to him about any progress.

Ponzi and Terra were most interested in the lead on the gun in Sheepshead Bay. When we returned to Brooklyn, we arranged with the NYPD scuba unit to search the area drawn on our pad by Casso. The divers did a thorough job, but even if the map accurately showed where Casso originally dumped the gun fifteen years ago, time and water currents had changed the bottom so much that no one expected the weapon to be found.

And we could not corroborate any of the other leads Casso gave us, although I do believe he was telling us the truth.

Chapter 14

Medical Terrorism

There is a sufficiency in the world for man's needs but not for man's greed.

—Mahatma Gandhi

AROUND THE TIME IN 2005 that Judge Barron was getting out of prison and we were knee-deep in the investigations of Judge Garson and political boss Norman, Josh Hanshaft—one of the best investigative prosecutors I have ever known, a stalwart of the Rackets Division—stuck his head in my office and asked if I could spare a few minutes.

I tried to never say no to such a request. That's how things got started in Rackets. I encouraged my team to bring me their ideas, suspicions, complaints, and goals. People from Frieda Hanimov to Greg Scarpa Jr. found the men and women of the Rackets Division willing to listen to what they had to say and to act on their behalf if necessary.

Josh was "riding" that day—that is, he was the Rackets prosecutor on call to handle any case that might show up in the lobby or come in by telephone, e-mail, or even from another lawyer, confidential informant, cop, or reporter over lunch. Even a judge or politician might pass on something that warranted at least a look.

During my career, I had dealt with a head found by a fisherman, a cop who posed for a nude magazine, a man who posed as his dead mother so he could collect her Social Security checks, a famous actor who punched out a bar bouncer, Chinese counterfeiting rings that sold everything from diapers to designer jeans, and even a rabbi who kidnapped a young boy because he believed he saw the light of the Messiah in the boy's eyes.

I had prosecuted a wiseguy who wanted to have sex with one of the witnesses testifying against him, a man. And I once defended a promising sculptor who fought her abusive husband by setting him on fire. When she had second thoughts, she tried to put the fire out, burning her hands so badly that she could never sculpt again.

But what I was about to learn from Josh that afternoon would take the *just when you thought you heard it all* prize for any prosecutor.

Josh sat down on the sofa across from my desk and took a deep breath. He said that a detective and a civilian were in his office who had a weird story. Clearly Josh was putting it together in his own mind before relating it to me.

I understood he was looking for guidance; otherwise, he would have been more definite, more or less explaining how he needed a detective or paralegal assigned to him to help him check something out.

He told me that a woman, Debora Johnson, had gone to the Sixty-Second Precinct to file a complaint against the former owners of the Daniel George and Son Funeral Home, in Bensonhurst, which she had just purchased. She was from Indiana, where she and her estranged husband, Robert Nelms, had a business that invested in funeral homes around the country. The couple had bought Daniel George from Joseph Nicelli for $1.5 million in 2003.

Shortly after the sale, Nelms and Johnson received complaints that funeral prepayments were not being honored. The deal in Bensonhurst included about $300,000 in prepaid funeral costs, money put up by people in advance to ensure they had proper funerals. When they died, the money was to be in the accounts of the funeral home to cover costs. But the buyers from Indiana could not find the money in any of the accounts Nicelli had turned over. Johnson thought she had been shortchanged by Nicelli and went to the police to find out what she could do about it.

At the precinct, Detective Patricia O'Brien was assigned to listen to Johnson's complaint. O'Brien's NYPD supervisors were suspicious and thought an explanation was needed, but they were on unfamiliar ground. They would be more comfortable if it were an armed robbery and the new owner had been pistol-whipped. They would know how to run down that culprit in a heartbeat. But this had the earmarks of a white-collar crime, embezzlement they thought. To their credit, rather than proceed in unknown territory, they ordered O'Brien to bring it to the Brooklyn DA's Rackets Division.

As Ms. Johnson recounted her story to Josh, she also mentioned, almost as an afterthought, some suspicions she had about something else that might be going on in the funeral home, but she was not sure what it was. She related how, while inspecting the building, she came upon men working in a room that she did not previously know existed. Two men, surrounded by surgical equipment, seemed to be hard at work over a corpse in a coffin, but the conditions did not seem right to her. For one thing, they were clearly not embalming the body, and it bothered her that no sanitary precautions were being taken. She went over to the coffin and felt the body's leg. She remembered that it felt "squishy." She asked the men what they were doing. They responded that they were taking bones from the bodies.

The hair on my neck was standing up when I heard the words "taking bones." I asked Josh if he thought the missing money might have something to do with the two guys who were taking the bones in this secret room. I didn't know how it could be connected, but it sure sent shivers up my spine. Josh felt the same way.

"Well, it may be old-fashioned embezzlement, but let's find out," I told him.

Josh asked me which way should he go: Should he concentrate on the possible larceny or this strange angle involving cutting-up corpses?

"Put the three hundred grand on the back burner for the time being. Let's find out what is going with the body parts." I told him I wanted to be on top of the investigation every step of the way. I would always find time during Norman and Garson to weigh in on this case.

I'd thought I seen everything during a colorful career, but now, body snatchers at work! Even in Brooklyn, it was hard to imagine. But if anyone could figure it out, it would be Josh Hanshaft and an assistant district attorney who shared his phenomenal ability to ferret out significant information from reams of paperwork, whom Josh enlisted for help, Patricia "Trish" McNeill.

Josh went back to his office and told Detective O'Brien and Ms. Johnson that I'd given the okay to move the investigation ahead. A big job lay ahead.

Joseph Nicelli came from a family with long ties to the funeral-home business in Brooklyn. He was known as a trade embalmer as he worked for many funeral directors and was himself a licensed funeral director. His industry contacts were widespread across the city and the country as he often arranged for the shipping of deceaseds to other cities for burial.

The investigators took a long look at Nicelli, and as Barron had led to Garson and Garson had led to Norman, they learned of a disgraced oral surgeon named Michael Mastromarino, whom Nicelli was doing business with. Mastromarino, at forty-two years old, was already a notorious figure in the medical community. A tall, handsome former college football player, he'd attended the University of Pittsburgh on a scholarship, and some thought he would have had a future as a professional if not for a severe ankle injury. Right out of dental school he began making a reputation for himself as a talented oral surgeon. He even collaborated on a book: *Smile: How Dental Implants Can Transform Your Life.*

He developed a lucrative practice and lived a high-flying lifestyle in a beautiful home in Fort Lee, New Jersey, with his wife and two sons. He would boast to friends that he made more than $1 million a year. But then he turned to Demerol to help get him through the demands of his fame and fortune. He became an addict and lost control of himself.

A malpractice suit against him alleged that he was so stoned on Demerol he fell asleep while working on a patient. Another suit claimed that while the patient was under anesthesia, Mastromarino passed out in his office bathroom and was found on the floor with a hypodermic needle. These kinds of suits and complaints from colleagues and patients led to the revocation of Mastromarino's dental license. He could no longer earn a living to support his family. He hit bottom but found a way to sink even lower.

During his days as an oral surgeon, Mastromarino had performed many surgeries using human tissue and bone taken from someone else and transplanted into the patient. Employing his medical knowledge and surgical skills, he created a company called Biomedical Tissue Services (BTS), a human-tissue-recovery firm. His idea was to work through funeral homes to find tissue donors among the recently deceased. He and his assistants would harvest the available tissue from the bodies, then sell it to larger firms that would process it for distribution to surgeons across the country.

The human tissue industry makes $1 billion a year. A single human body can be worth more than $100,000 in harvested tissue. Bones, veins, tendons, and other parts can be used in bypass surgery and to repair fractured bones and for many other uses, including dental implants. For instance, bones can be turned into plates and screws.

Mastromarino recruited funeral home operators such as Joseph Nicelli to supply him with bodies, offering $1,000 a body. This was perfectly legal. Tissue harvesting is allowed in New York State as long as the deceased has given permission or a surviving family member consents and the deceased did not have HIV, a communicable disease, cancer, or was too old. Mastromarino had found a way to restore his life in the fast lane.

The only trouble was, as Josh and Trish found out, that when the funeral home operators approached the bereaved families on behalf of Mastromarino's BTS, their answers were a resounding no. Surviving spouses and children did not want their loved ones chopped to pieces and divided up into body parts, even if they had already planned on cremation. That put Mastromarino in a jam and led to his plan B, which turned him into one of the most notorious criminals in New York history. He became known in the tabloids as a "ghoul, body snatcher and monster."

As the Rackets team and NYPD Major Case Squad dug deeper, they learned more, and their reports back to me sounded increasingly macabre. In the early 1800s in London, doctors were pioneering surgical procedures and learning more and more about the mysteries of the human body and how to repair damage caused by injury or disease. Much of their research necessitated the use of cadavers, preferably recently deceased local citizens. The legal supply of bodies, mostly of executed criminals, could not keep pace with the demand from the medical schools.

The need created a financial opportunity for those willing to work as body snatchers, grave robbers, or, as they were more politely known, resurrectionists. The practice led to at least one infamous case of murder and a sensational trial when two Scotsmen, William Burke and William Hare, were arrested for committing sixteen murders in order to sell the victims' bodies to Dr. Robert Knox in Edinburgh, who conducted important anatomy lessons using the cadavers. Hare turned "king's evidence" and testified against Burke, who went to the gallows. Dr. Knox was never criminally charged.

Those were the kind of discussions we were having about this case when I was briefed by Hanshaft and McNeill. It was like being in the middle of an episode of *The Twilight Zone.*

We searched through thousands of documents, including consent forms allowing donations of tissue. We had detectives going door-to-door throughout the city, wherever BTS had connections to funeral homes. The detectives would knock on the doors without prior notice, show the forms, and ask directly if permission was granted. When we took those documents to surviving family members whose signatures appeared on the permission line, we learned every time that those signatures were forged. No one ever gave permission.

BTS's business plan: No permission, no problem; communicable disease, HIV, no problem; age of deceased, doesn't matter. Ship off the tissue to the tissue-processing companies all over the world. Collect $4 million a year.

Mastromarino had found a new, lucrative business.

Tissue-processing companies required a sample of blood from the deceased to accompany the tissue to ensure it met their requirements regarding communicable diseases and cancer. To trick the companies Mastromarino carried a bag with him filled with "clean" blood samples. He would use those vials to send along with the stolen body parts.

When we got warrants to search his Fort Lee house and garage, we found freezers packed with body parts and blood samples. Mastromarino made Burke and Hale look like pikers.

We heard a story about a grief-stricken widow who at the funeral of her husband wanted to touch him for the last time. She reached into his coffin, and instead of feeling flesh and bone, she described what she felt as "pipe." We discovered that Mastromarino and the two men working for him would cut out the bones of deceased and replace them with PVC pipe. That was the acceptable procedure when the tissue harvesting was done within the law, but Mastromarino was a heartless outlaw operating by his own rules and without concern for anything but making money. To me, he seemed more evil than any killer or sex fiend that I had ever sent to prison.

When I told Hynes what we were finding, or when I briefed the press office, they just sat openmouthed in astonishment over what was going on. The reaction of the loved ones was always the same: revulsion, disgust, and determination that the ghouls responsible be brought to justice, although some had their own definition of what justice should be.

Before we stopped them, we figured Mastromarino's ring plundered more than fourteen hundred bodies and sold the body parts, which were subsequently distributed to about twenty thousand recipients from 2001 to 2005. Much of that dirty work was done in the secret room on the second floor at Daniel George Funeral Home, where Ms. Johnson discovered two of BTS's employees hard at work with saws and knives, PVC pipe, and duct tape.

The room had an elevator platform that lifted the bodies from the garage below after they were driven there by hearse from other funeral homes, homes of the deceased, and hospitals. The lift was so carefully designed that if you looked at the garage floor, you would have no clue that the apparatus was there. The operation was more bizarre to me than Gaspipe Casso's revelation that he threw Jimmy Hydell's body in front of a bulldozer and it was plowed under a housing development.

On October 6, 2005, my press office got a call from Pulitzer Prize–winning reporter William Sherman of the *New York Daily News*. He said he had a story about a Brooklyn-based body-snatching ring run by a New Jersey dentist. He said he was not looking for information, but was just being courteous letting us know he had the story of our investigation and asking if we wanted to comment.

The DA's spokesman knew about our investigation and felt out Sherman to see just how much he knew. No prosecutor wants to read about his case in the newspapers before he is ready to make it public. Revelations like that can panic witnesses, scare victims, or, most important, alert suspects that we are onto them.

That kind of leak to a journalist can come from many sources. It could have been one of my prosecutors or detectives, or sometimes a determined reporter can dig out a court record of a motion or warrant that opens a door to further questions.

I suspected Sherman had got his information from a lawyer for one of the witnesses or family members we had now spent about one year questioning. Sometimes a reporter will cooperate and hold off publishing until we can get the suspect into custody or at least, through his lawyer, have some assurance he will not flee. But our spokesman told me Sherman would probably not hold back the story because he seemed to have it complete. He did not need information from us, just a comment if we wanted to make it. The spokesman suggested I meet with Sherman to find out what he had.

We arranged a meeting and I was convinced Sherman had a solid story, based on fact and with few errors. Rather than have erroneous information out there, I offered some suggestions, and the next day when the story ran, I thought it was accurate, but not complete.

None of the suspects fled after the story appeared. We were ready to pick them up if they tried, and our investigation continued. But now, the investigation was known to the public, and the pressure to solve it increased as the media became as fascinated with the case as the Rackets Division had been.

A few days after Sherman's article, the Food and Drug Administration ordered a recall of body parts received from companies that dealt with Mastromarino. The ghoul's victims now included people who'd got tissue and bone from his company.

We had a good handle on the case, understood what it was all about, and had a trial strategy in mind that would prove Mastromarino's guilt to a jury.

But Josh came to me with a wise precaution. He pointed out, correctly, that all we had was what people told us: "Don't you think we need to see it for ourselves, to see if it is true?"

He was correct. I asked him what he had in mind, and he answered that bodies needed to be exhumed. That was the only way to get undeniable proof. That was an excruciating thought.

It meant that we would have to go back to the family members of the deceased to allow us to dig up the graves of their loved ones. They had already been outraged over the forgeries, the cuttings, the lying. Now they had to relive it. The court requires family permission to exhume a body. There was no way around it. The cemetery operators will not let you near a grave without that court order.

I agonized over this decision. A prosecutor always walks a fine line in dealing with survivors. You ask embarrassing, sometimes humiliating questions about people they loved. You put them on the spot, often asking them to do things that go against their nature. This was one of those times. But Josh raised an important issue. Why should we come all this way and not finish the jobs? I agreed with him and we exhumed six bodies.

The media got wind of what we were doing, and on one occasion a news helicopter hovered overhead as cemetery workers, with Josh looking on, went about their grisly business. During one of the exhumations, the coffin tilted as it was being lifted from the grave and the body slipped out. I'm glad no press helicopter was overhead when that happened.

As emotionally trying as exhuming those bodies was, it turned out to be worth the effort. In each of the six exhumed bodies we found PVC pipe in place of bones. We took X-rays of it all. That would become damning evidence.

We did not want to rush arrests and indictments, but we and the police were now getting calls to make something happen. How long were we going to let these ghouls walk the streets? Also, more survivors who wondered about the fate of their loved ones began calling our office. As is my practice, I ordered each lead checked out.

One of the survivors we contacted was Susan Cooke Kittredge, the daughter of Alistair Cooke. The iconic British broadcaster had been admired in America as host of *Masterpiece Theatre* on PBS and in his native Great Britain for his *Letter from America* which ran on BBC Radio for sixty years. Our investigation revealed that in 2004 Cooke died of cancer at age ninety-five. His family arranged through a Mastromarino-connected funeral home in Manhattan for his body to be cremated in a New Jersey facility. Without his family's knowledge or permission Cooke's leg bones were removed from his body and sold to a tissue-processing company for $11,000. BTS forged the necessary documents to make it appear he was a suitable donor by stating the cause of death was a heart attack and he was eighty-four years old.

When we first approached Kittredge, she told us she had some suspicions after she scattered her father's ashes. She said she remembered the ashes being powdery, not gritty as she'd expected, and without signs of any bones. Now she understood why! Kittredge told us and later testified under oath that her father was absolutely against being an organ donor. She told reporters he did not like the idea of being cut up.

At the end of 2005, the investigation began winding down, and we began showing evidence to a grand jury. The evidence included X-rays of PVC pipe in place of bones in the legs of corpses. You could clearly see the nuts and bolts they used to fix the pipe to the remaining human bones. Also, the forged documents, diagrams of the secret room on the second floor of the Daniel George, and expert testimony on the use of bone and tissue were presented.

On February 23, 2006, we held a press conference at our building to announce the indictments of Mastromarino, Nicelli, and the two bone cutters, Lee Crucetta and Christopher Aldorasi. The press conference room was SRO, the biggest turnout of press we ever accommodated. All the advance stories had the world's media foaming at the bit for this day. More than twenty-five television stations from around the world covered the event, and at least two broadcast live from our nineteenth-floor press conference room. NYPD commissioner Raymond Kelly and the commissioner of the Department of Investigation, Rose Gill Hearn, joined DA Hynes, me, Josh Hanshaft, Trish McNeill, a half dozen assistant prosecutors, and dozens of Major Case Squad detectives, DA investigators, paralegals, and other support staff at the podium.

If you measure big cases in terms of the exposure they receive, this was the biggest. At least three major networks here and in Great Britain produced documentaries on the case. A few years later when we were approached by CBS's star producer Susan Zirinsky for permission to produce a six-part documentary series on our office, she cited the "Bones" case as one of our great accomplishments.

I arraigned the four defendants in supreme court that afternoon on charges of enterprise corruption, body stealing, opening graves, unlawful dissection, and forgery. In front of Judge John Walsh, I accused Mastromarino and his crew of engaging in "medical terrorism." Mastromarino was held on $1.5 million bail, the kind of sum a killer is held on. Nicelli's bail was $250,000, and Crucetta and Aldorasi, the two who got their hands dirty, $500,000 each.

In the years that followed only Aldorasi chose to go to trial and was found guilty and sentenced to nine to twenty-seven years in prison. He argued he believed Mastromarino had cleared everything with survivors and he just followed the boss's orders. He would have done a little better if he'd pled guilty like Nicelli and Crucetta; they got eight to twenty-four years each.

On March 19, 2008, the once-admired dentist from New Jersey, former collegiate football star, and millionaire, pled guilty to running his corrupt enterprise, reaping $4.6 million a year in illicit profits derived from selling body parts of the recently deceased. Wearing jeans and a freshly pressed shirt, Mastromarino sat impassively as Josh Hanshaft read the names of twenty-four people whose bodies were carved up without permission.

As Josh and Trish read the more than one hundred counts of the indictment detailing his crimes, he answered, "Yes," each time when asked if he pled guilty. The harrowing court session lasted more than an hour.

In return for his admissions, he received a sentence of eighteen to fifty-four years in prison. In the gallery, his family absorbed the confession that he had knowingly sold tissue that was cancerous or infected with HIV and hepatitis, and he'd covered that up by lying about the cause of death on the paperwork. After Mastromarino was led away, his lawyer, Mario Gallucci, conceded to reporters in the hallway that his client "decided to cut corners to satisfy the increasing demand for business."

Josh followed that up with one of the best rejoinders I have ever heard. He said Mastromarino cut more than corners: "He cut limbs, he cut legs, he cut arms. He mutilated bodies for profit and greed."

In 2012, Mastromarino sat for a prison interview with journalists. They concluded that, like many convicted criminals, he blamed everyone but himself for the wreck his life became. "They made me out to be, like, I was doing something completely outrageous. Secret rooms . . . bodies being ripped apart. I mean that's simply not the case," he told the reporters in the face of the evidence that sent him to prison. Charges also would be brought against Mastromarino in Rochester, New York, New Jersey, and Pennsylvania.

But in the most classic case of *what goes around comes around* I have ever encountered, we got news during the summer of 2013 that Mastromarino was being treated in a prison hospital for bone cancer. He died on July 7, 2013, at the age of forty-nine.

Epilogue

A FEW YEARS after Mastromarino was sent off to prison but before he died, I was invited to appear on a show being produced by the Lifetime network for a series on wives who married bad guys.

I reported to their studio on the West Side of Manhattan about 4:00 p.m. as requested. It was a difficult place to find. I had to ask someone in the street for directions, and I ended up in a huge warehouse-type building that seemed empty to me.

A worker told me I was in the right place and pointed me down a long, dimly lit passageway. At the end was a soda machine and two small sofas facing each other. I thought this cold atmosphere was fitting for a show about a monster.

As I approached the sofas, I noticed a woman sitting with her back toward me. I politely asked her if I was in the right place.

"You're Mike Vecchione, right?"

I said I was. "Who are you?"

"I'm Barbra Mastromarino, although now I'm known as Barbra Mastro."

As soon as she said it, I realized she was Mastromarino's wife. I remember seeing her in court at one of the hearings. An attractive woman, she stood out in the gallery.

I was uncomfortable meeting her in these circumstances. After all, I was somewhat responsible for taking her husband from his family. My staff portrayed him as one of the greatest fiends in criminal history. It could not have made her happy. I figured she hated me.

"Mike, I want you to know that I hold nothing against you. My husband was a monster. I had no idea what kind of man I was married to." She knew her husband had overcome serious problems that had caused him to lose his license to practice dentistry.

She said that one day her life was great, "and the next day it completely fell apart." She told me how she had to change her name to get on with her life. She was left penniless, and their multimillion-dollar house in Fort Lee was seized to make reparations to the families of victims. I admired her spirit. She was not going to let her husband's failures destroy her.

I told her I was there to do an interview for a show about the case. She said she was also being interviewed, and her son was in front of the cameras right then.

"My son does not feel the same way I do," she said. "He will not change his name, and he visits his father in jail. He's very loyal, but it tears him apart inside. I don't think he would be so happy to meet you. When he comes out, I am not going to introduce you."

Then she stunned me by thanking me for what I had done. "It needed to be done. It saved our family." When the son came out, we avoided each other, and I was called into the room where they were doing the interviews.

Driving back to Brooklyn, I kept replaying the encounter with Barbra Mastro. *There I was,* I thought, *sitting with the enemy, and she thanked me.*

I've had other unusual encounters with close family members of defendants I prosecuted. A killer's mother cursed me out in the courtroom and threatened to kill me, but a few months later asked a mutual friend if I would be interested in dating her. Maybe she wanted to get close enough to poison me. I rejected the offer.

The father of a murdered cop wrote a hate-filled letter to me after the killer was acquitted. I understood he just needed someone to vent to, but it still hurt me as I had worked hard and was satisfied I had done the best I could.

I was treated like a hero in the Orthodox Jewish community after I convicted the killer of a young mother.

Those kinds of things happen to all prosecutors. But I wondered as I drove that night if we, prosecutors, understand the collateral damage we cause by doing our jobs. I wonder if we think enough about the maelstrom we become the center of when we enter the world of defendants, witnesses, victims, and innocent bystanders such as families. It bothers me, but it cannot be helped. The important thing is not to lose sight of those implications. We serve the greater needs of society.

I warn my students to not become too hardened. They should not ignore people who depend on them. They need to respect everyone involved, even the defendants.

But I also tell them not to fear the big cases. They should not shy away from a case where the world might be watching and might be judging them. As my dad would say to me, "Do the right thing and you will never regret your decisions."

The Bones case is still a subject of fascination for the media, and not much time goes by that I don't get a call for information or a request for an interview about it. That case capped a remarkable period in my career. From 2001 through 2008, I was responsible for bringing three supreme court judges, one of the most powerful political bosses in the country, two cops who worked as assassins for the Mafia, a state assemblywoman, a controversial FBI agent, and a body snatcher before the court of justice. The success brought us to the attention of CBS News, which produced a six-part documentary called *Brooklyn DA,* which covered some of the cases and others that did not get as much publicity.

The Rackets Division was represented in the show with depictions of a case against an arsonist who killed four people, a doctor whose patient died after he performed liposuction on her even though she had undergone a heart transplant and was not cleared for that kind of surgery, and an art thief who preyed on the estate of a prominent Long Island family.

It was plenty to be proud of for sure. And I have plenty of people to thank for making it all possible. The Kings County District Attorney's Office in Brooklyn, New York, employs the finest prosecutors, detectives, paralegals, clerks, and technicians I have ever met.

My sister, Pamela, succumbed to her illness on July 12, 2009, at the age of fifty-five, and my father passed away September 11, 2011. He was ninety.

I was surrounded by controversy during my last two years in the office. Mostly it was about a man who was convicted of murder who sued the city after his conviction was vacated. His wrongheaded lawyer blamed the conviction on misconduct by me, even though no facts supported his argument. He made sure my name was connected to every negative story that came out of the Brooklyn DA's office. Well, I never ran from controversy. This was the big leagues. You can't put yourself out there without being exposed to criticism, sometimes undeserved. But that is where I belonged. I would not trade being Rackets chief for any other job on the planet.

District Attorney Hynes lost his bid for reelection for a seventh term in November 2013. There is no other district attorney I cared to work for, so in December I retired. My time will be spent teaching, mentoring, trying to pass on the lessons I learned over forty years as a prosecutor and criminal defense lawyer. Stay tuned.

Acknowledgments

The authors would like to thank our agent, Frank Weimann, for his encouragement and support, and Tom Dunne, Will Anderson, Rob Kirkpatrick, Jennifer Letwack, and the rest of the team at St. Martin's for their openness to our desire to tell this story. Morty Matz helped us in so many ways and continues to be a great friend to this project, and most of all thanks to Sheldon Shuch, PhD, whose guidance, honesty, and friendship were invaluable to our efforts.

The authors would also like to thank the great staff at Starbucks on Eighty-Fifth and First, New York City, for their hospitality at our "office" away from home.

Michael Vecchione acknowledges the following people: Uncle Louie, my mentor, who provided me with the support and encouragement to attend law school and enter this great profession; Uncle Fred, my godfather and my music teacher, who was always there for me with support, encouragement, and laughter. Their sons, my cousins Louis and Michael, for keeping the memory and spirit of their dads and our family alive; Aunt Jo, my second mom. Nothing else needs to be said. . . .

Jimmy Murphy, a great detective who brought me into the DA's office and whose stories and exploits inspired me to become Rackets chief . . . Joe Petrosino, my great friend and partner in Rackets. We had a great run! Chief Joe Ponzi, for his selfless contributions to the cases in this book. The great George Terra and the men and women of the Special Investigations Unit, for their unbelievable work and dedication to these cases and countless others. We kicked some ass! And for keeping me safe! . . . The men and women of the Rackets Division mentioned in this book. You are the best! . . . Frances Mercurio, my wonderful assistant and partner from day one in Rackets. She did it all for me, kept me grounded, focused, and encouraged in the face of much adversity and pressure. She brightened every day she was with me. None of what I've chronicled in this book would have been possible without her. God bless her!

And Jerry Schmetterer, my partner, my coauthor, and most important my great friend!

Jerry Schmetterer acknowledges Emily Schmetterer for her encouragement and support for this project and all that preceded it over a lot of 24-7 years. The encouragement of all my family, David and Nina Schmetterer, Charlie and Christel Alaimo, was so important to me at this time in my career. Wayne and Eden Winderman were great sounding boards, and thanks to my cousin Annette Georgios for her support, encouragement, and honesty. I appreciate them all. Most important I would like to thank my friend Mike Vecchione for his willingness to share his thoughts about a remarkable career.

Awards

Michael F. Vecchione has received many awards over his career, including:

- Distinguished Alumnus Award—2008
Hofstra University School of Law

- Robert N. Kaye Award—2008
Kings County Criminal Bar Association

- Thomas E. Dewey Medal—2007
Association of the Bar of the City of New York

- "Home Run Hitters" Hall of Fame Award—2003
National District Attorneys Association

- Linda Mills Memorial Community Service Award—2000
New York State Division of Parole

- Award of Appreciation—2000
New York City Fire Department, Fire Marshals

- Certificate of Appreciation—1998
New York City Fire Department

- City Council Citation—1996
New York City Council

- Certificate of Appreciation—1996
Sixty-Eighth Precinct (NYPD) Community Council

- Brooklyn Borough President Citation—1992